NARRATIVES OF (DIS)ENGAGEMENT

Exploring Black and African American Students' Experiences in Libraries

**AMANDA L. FOLK AND
TRACEY OVERBEY**

ALA
Editions

CHICAGO 2022

ALA Editions purchases fund advocacy, awareness, and accreditation programs for library professionals worldwide.

© 2022 by Amanda L. Folk and Tracey Overbey

ISBNs
978-0-8389-4886-6 (paper)
978-0-8389-4993-1 (PDF)

Library of Congress Cataloging-in-Publication Data

Names: Folk, Amanda L., author. | Overbey, Tracey, author.
Title: Narratives of (dis)engagement : exploring Black and African American students' experiences in libraries / Amanda L. Folk and Tracey Overbey.
Description: Chicago : ALA Editions, 2022. | Series: ALA Editions special reports | Includes bibliographical references and index. | Summary: "In this report, the authors introduce the findings of a research study that explores Black and African American students' experiences with libraries, examining the role that race has played in these students' library experiences to identify potential opportunities for libraries to better meet the needs of these users" —Provided by publisher.
Identifiers: LCCN 2022018690 (print) | LCCN 2022018691 (ebook) | ISBN 9780838948866 (paperback) | ISBN 9780838949931 (pdf)
Subjects: LCSH: Libraries and Black people—United States. | African Americans and libraries.
Classification: LCC Z711.9 .F65 2022 (print) | LCC Z711.9 (ebook) | DDC 027.0089/96073—dc23/eng/20220521
LC record available at https://lccn.loc.gov/2022018690
LC ebook record available at https://lccn.loc.gov/2022018691

Series cover design by Casey Bayer. Series text design in Palatino Linotype and Interstate by Karen Sheets de Gracia.

♾ This paper meets the requirements of ANSI/NISO Z39.48-1992 (Permanence of Paper).

Printed in the United States of America
26 25 24 23 22   5 4 3 2 1

CONTENTS

PREFACE

"Being American is more than a pride we inherit, it's the past we step into and how we repair it."—Amanda Gorman, *The Hill We Climb*

"I can't breathe."—Eric Garner

"Mama."—George Floyd

We believe it's important to place this book within our country's broader racial context, as it is this context that has inspired us to write this book and encourage our profession to consider what it means to confront racism in our libraries and communities and develop actionable antiracist agendas. We began this project in earnest in 2017. According to #Say Their Names (https://sayevery .name), eight Black and African American children and adults in six different states ranging in age from 15 to 66 were murdered by law enforcement or died in police custody that year. Damon Grimes. James Lacy. Charleena Lyles. Mikel McIntyre. Jordan Edwards. Timothy Caughman. Alteria Woods. Desmond Phillips. In 2018 that number almost doubled. Fourteen Black and African American children and adults in eight states ranging in age from 17 to 45 were murdered by law enforcement or died in police custody. Aleah Jenkins. Emantic Bradford Jr. Jemel Robinson. Charles Roundtree Jr. Botham Jean. Harith Augustus. Jason Washington. Antwon Rose Jr. Robert White. Earl McNeil. Marcus-David Peters. Danny Ray Thomas. Stephon Clark. Ronell Foster. In 2019 eleven Black and African American adults in seven different states ranging in age from 21 to 56 were murdered by law enforcement or died in police custody. John Neville. Michael Dean. Atatiana Jeff-erson. Byron Williams. Elijah McClain. Jaleel Murdock. Dominique Clayton. Pamela Turner. Ronald Greene. Sterling Higgins. Bradley Blackshire. In 2019 a 66-year-old Atlanta librarian was pulled over in North Carolina for going 10 miles per hour over the speed limit. She did not realize that the police were attempting to pull her over, and they interpreted this as her attempting to run from them. When she realized what was happening and pulled over, officers pulled her out of her vehicle by her hair and threw her to the ground with their guns drawn on the side of the highway. All of this was caught on body camera video. At one point, one of the officers can be heard saying, "That's good police work, baby." So good that Ms. Bottom suffered a dislocated shoulder and torn rotator cuff that required surgery. At the time of writing, Ms. Bottom has filed a lawsuit against Salisbury (NC) City Police.

We decided to develop a book proposal to submit to ALA Editions in the summer of 2020. As we witnessed yet another unarmed Black man murdered by the police—George Floyd—and how the ensuing protests were met with militarized police forces across the country, we decided that writing this book was one small step that we could take in the fight for racial justice. Indeed, in Columbus, Ohio, we watched video footage of our own Black elected officials, including Congresswoman Joyce Beatty and City Council President Shannon Hardin, being pepper sprayed by the Columbus Division of Police as they exercised their First Amendment rights on public sidewalks downtown. Furthermore, we were in the midst of a global pandemic that was disproportionately affecting Black and African American communities. Due to a variety of factors, such as continued unequal access to health care, implicit bias in the provision of health care, and their overrepresentation in jobs considered to be essential, Black Americans and African Americans were 2.4 times more likely than White Americans to die as a result of COVID-19, according to an article published by the National Academies of Sciences, Engineering, and Medicine in July 2020 (Frueh, 2020).

As 2020 continued to unfold, the picture did not become more positive. Thirty-one Black and African American adults in 19 different states ranging in age from 18 to 60 were murdered by law enforcement or died in police custody. Bennie Edwards. Casey Goodson Jr. Kevin Peterson. Walter Wallace Jr. Jonathan Price. Kurt Reinhold. Dijon Kizzee. Damian Daniels. Anthony McClain. Julian Lewis. Maurice Abisdid-Wagner. Rayshard Brooks. Priscilla Slater. Kamal Flowers. Jamel Floyd. David McAtee. Calvin Horton Jr. Tony McDade. Dion Johnson. George Floyd. Maurice Gordon. Steven Taylor. Daniel Prude. Breonna Taylor. Barry Gedeus. Manuel Ellis. Lionel Morris. Jaquyn O'Neill Light. William Green. Darius Tarver. Miciah Lee. This list does not include Ahmaud Arbery, who was followed and murdered by White men in Georgia while he was out for a run. It took 74 days for an arrest to be made despite video evidence. This list also does not include Andre Hill, who was murdered by a Columbus (OH) police officer in his own driveway near the end of 2020. In between those two murders, a grand jury failed to indict the police officer who murdered Breonna Taylor as she slept in her own home.

We began a semester-long research leave to focus our energies on writing this book in January 2021, and 2021 seems to have been a continuation of 2020 in many ways. On the same day that Andre Hill was laid to rest—January 5, 2021—the Kenosha County (WI) District Attorney announced that they would not file charges against the officer who murdered Jacob Blake. The following day crowds of Trump supporters, who are predominantly White, began to gather at the Capitol in Washington, DC, to protest the certification of the presidential election results. Even though there was advance warning of protests, the footage showed very little law enforcement present, a remarkable contrast to protests across the country in support of Black lives and racial justice, which were often met with scores of police in riot gear and occasionally the National Guard. A failed insurrection at the Capitol ensued. On April 20, 2021, the officer who murdered George Floyd was found guilty on three counts—second-degree unintentional murder, second-degree manslaughter, and third-degree manslaughter. Even though this verdict could not bring George Floyd back to life, many celebrated the fact that a police officer was finally being held to account for murdering a Black man. This celebration was short-lived, as a Columbus (OH) police officer killed 16-year-old Ma'Khia Bryant while she was in an altercation that included a knife. Just hours following her death, there was video footage of other Columbus (OH) police officers telling neighborhood residents that blue lives matter. While there has been controversy about whether or not her death was warranted (it was not), because she had a knife, it stands in stark contrast to a long list of White men who have committed mass murders and were peacefully taken into custody even while heavily armed. The day after that, Andre Brown Jr. was killed by police officers in Elizabeth City, North Carolina, while sitting in his vehicle in his driveway with his hands on the steering wheel. At the time of writing, 10 additional Black and African American adults in eight different states ranging in age from 18 to 52 have already been murdered by law enforcement or died in police custody. Matthew "Zadok" Williams. Daunte Wright. James Lionel Johnson. Dominique Williams. Marvin Scott III. Jenoah Donald. Patrick Warren. Xzavier Hill. Robert Howard. Vincent Belmonte.

Through our complementary special reports, the one that follows and *Narratives of (Dis)Enfranchisement: Reckoning with the History of Libraries and the Black and African American Experience,* we hope to demonstrate the ways in which both systemic racism and implicit bias affect our profession. Many like to tout libraries as neutral spaces because we uphold the ideals of democracy and provide free access to all. However, libraries are not neutral spaces, and the reproduction of that narrative results in unequal service to different user populations. As is explained in more depth in our companion report, *Narratives of (Dis)Enfranchisement*, libraries and the institutions with which they are associated have a long history of racial exclusion. Furthermore, as we discuss in this report, few studies have explored the ways in which the legacy of that exclusion manifests in contemporary libraries for those who are Black, Indigenous, and People of Color (BIPOC). These complementary special reports are an initial attempt at filling that gap, beginning a conversation, and creating a call to action.

One of the authors, Tracey, once heard a trainer offering an equity, diversity, and inclusion workshop say something like, "Who owns the earth? We all have to breathe." As a profession, we need to make sure that we are providing environments that offer for all of our diverse user populations and professional colleagues the space to breathe and to thrive.

ACKNOWLEDGMENTS

Many people directly or indirectly made this report a reality, and we would like to take some space to say thank you to them.

FROM BOTH TRACEY AND AMANDA

We thank Damon Jaggars, Vice Provost and Dean of The Ohio State University Libraries, for providing us with funding to conduct this research study, as well as a special assignment for both of us to concentrate our energies on writing this special report. We thank Damon also for his unwavering support for this project in general and for providing us with a safe environment in which to do this work. We also thank our supervisors, Deidra Herring and Alison Armstrong, for their unconditional support of research and writing related to this project, including allowing us to apply for and take a special assignment in 2021. We thank our University Libraries colleagues more generally for encouraging our research and scholarship related to this topic.

We thank several colleagues for providing us with thoughtful and useful feedback on early drafts of chapters—Dr. Renee Hill, Dr. Sandra Hughes-Hassell, Dr. Kafi Kumasi, Nichole Shabazz, and Shaunda Vasudev. We appreciate the time, labor, and expertise that you were willing to share with us. We also thank the Tulsa City-County Library Research Center, particularly Nick Abrahamson, for their willingness to provide us with documentation related to the Tulsa Race Massacre and the Archer Street Library.

Finally, we thank our acquisitions editor at ALA Editions, Rachel Chance, for enthusiastically believing in our project and providing us with guidance and feedback throughout this process. If it were not for Rachel, this special report would not be a reality. We are grateful for your support!

FROM TRACEY

Participating in this type of study has shed so much light, providing insight into and awareness of the many contributions and struggles of people of Black and African American ancestry and their contributions to society and the world that have gone hidden, unnoticed, and unacknowledged. I would like to honor known and unknown Black and African American ancestors who created civilizations and institutions, who went unacknowledged for their contributions to the world. I would like to say thank you for setting a blueprint for many civilizations to follow.

I thank my colleague, research partner, and coauthor, Dr. Amanda Folk, for being brave, inquisitive, and bold enough to peer inside a little bit of what has been hidden within Black and African American ancestry history. You have viewed and examined the research, more than most have done, and have been humble enough to acknowledge it within our publication. I am very grateful for you reaching out to me, in a setting that had only a few who looked like me, to ask if we could work together on a very sensitive topic like race and libraries. My hope is that the information which we have shared will be continued in academic librarianship by new and upcoming librarians—who will be just as brave and honest as you have been to uncover those hidden truths about the Black and African American experiences with libraries.

I thank my mother, Annie Mcgrady, for her absolute devotion in guiding me toward education and seeking knowledge. You explained to me very early how the world sees our people and how I must change that narrative through education. You have been a great example for me to follow. I appreciate all the many settings you placed me in that had many races and ethnicities. I truly appreciate the sacrifices and love you have shown me throughout my life. I also thank my dad, Wash Allen; I thank you for being my secret motivator! You have always lit the fire in me to keep me going when I wanted to give up. I am ever grateful for being your daughter and for the love you have shown me through my life.

I thank my husband, my best friend and confidant, Edward E. Overbey Jr. You have always supported me—on every venture I conjure. I appreciate all the encouragement, spiritual insights, and love. You champion me when no one sees the struggle; you are a fantastic partner and an excellent father and human being; a woman could not ask for more in a mate. I would also like to acknowledge my children, Rodney Maurice Williams Jr and Asa Khalil Overbey. Rodney, although you transitioned at a young age, I know you are my angel, watching over me and helping me along my life purpose. I miss you so much; not a day goes by that I do not think about you and feel your spirit. Asa, I'm so grateful you chose me to be your mother; it has been an honor to raise you and watch you grow into this bright, funny, loving engineer that you want to become. Please know this is all for you, and my grandchildren one day.

I would also like to shout out family members who have passed on, but who are never forgotten and whose shoulders I stand on today. My grandparents Chester and Annie Ruth Mcgrady, who taught me consistency and perseverance. To my late uncle bug, Chester Mcgrady Jr, Cynthia Horton (auntie), Lawrence and Brian Adam Mcgrady (cousins), and last but not least my great-great grandmother (big ma) Sallie Mcgrady. To my living family and friends who have stood by me in test of times during this journey. My brother, Michael McCall, I appreciate you always

reaching out and encouraging me and my family to strive higher and be the best we can be. My dear sister, Wykema Morse, I have watched you over time, you inspire me so much; I love you so dearly. To my dear friend since elementary school Monica Daniely, we have cried and achieved together, I appreciate the honest and empowering talks. Last but not least, my dearest friend Kimberly Granger-Cummings (my ride or die), although we don't talk often, I truly appreciate the support you have given me throughout this journey called life. I truly miss you.

I also thank mentors in my life who have encouraged me on this journey in academia. Dr. Rena Mae Baker, you have been a great mentor, and role model, who encourages me often that I can do this, and that my experiences are needed within the scholarship arena for academic libraries. Deidra Herring, I truly appreciate your leadership in sparking the fire in me through academic libraries.

FROM AMANDA

I first thank my research partner and coauthor, Tracey Overbey. I don't know what it was that made you trust me when I suggested this research project, but I will be eternally grateful to you for taking this risk. Our research has been one of the high points of my career, and I believe our shared accomplishments will be those of which I am most proud. This work has been some of the most meaningful and rewarding work of my career. It was not your responsibility to educate me, but I have learned so much from you that has made me a better librarian and person. I thank you so much for your willingness to work together, and I'm really looking forward to shaping our next project together!

I thank my parents, Dan and Cindy Folk, for your unconditional love and support in everything that I do, personally and professionally. While I have a lot of growth to do as an antiracist and White ally, you taught me from an early age that it is important to have friends who are different from you. As I reflect on my own experiences, being in a diverse day care setting was foundational, as some of the earliest friends that I can remember making were African

American or biracial. I didn't realize how unusual that was until I was much older.

I thank my husband and best friend, Allen Perry. You believe in me more than I believe in myself, and you support me even when I take on projects that require so much of me that there is little left of me to devote to other things. Thank you for always being there for me, telling me that I am capable of accomplishing my goals, keeping my feet on the ground, reminding me to take a moment to breathe, and for learning alongside me.

I thank Dr. Linda DeAngelo, not only for being an amazing mentor, but also for modeling what it means to be an antiracist scholar and White ally. You have given me the tools to embark on this journey, and I wouldn't be the scholar that I am today without you. I am so grateful for you and your continued support.

I'm also fortunate to have so many close friends and colleagues who have helped me along this journey as mentors and peers in the learning process. Thank you so much to Maria Accardi, Dr. Sheila Confer, Sandra Enimil, Pamela Espinosa de los Monteros, Jenn Grimmett, Pema Lin, Marley Nelson, Z Tenney, Dr. Erika Pryor, Jessica Riviere, and (last, but definitely not least!) Dr. Gretchen Underwood-Schaefer. I also thank my running besties who shared many miles with me throughout this process—Tom Anderson, Jess Moomaw, Morgan Myers, Becca Rohner, and Renata Weaver.

INTRODUCTION

THE ORIGIN STORY

Within a couple of months of arriving at Ohio State, Amanda attended her first Focusing on the First Year Conference offered by the university's First Year Experience unit. The first breakout session that she attended was a panel about stigmas rwelated to Black males and masculinity called "Narratives of Black Undergraduate Men: Manhood, Masculinities, and the First-Year Experience," which was organized by Mr. Tai Cornute and Dr. Christopher S. Travers.[1] After providing an overview of research and scholarship related to this topic, four Black male Ohio State students spoke honestly and bravely about how they wrestle with stigmas related to Black masculinity as college students. One of the topics addressed was seeking help and how it is stigmatized as a weakness, not a strength. Having staffed a reference desk for many years prior to coming to Ohio State, Amanda found that this discussion caused her to think about how the reference desk and research consultations might be inaccessible to Black male students, something that she, as a White woman, had not previously considered. In addition, Amanda started to think about how this may be compounded by the fact that academic librarianship, as a profession, is predominantly White and female. How then can we, as a profession and as individual librarians, serve Black and African American library users whose identities are disturbingly underrepresented among our ranks and who may view reaching out to library employees for help as showing signs of weakness?

Not too long after this, we (Amanda and Tracey) had our first onboarding meeting, as we were both new to our positions, to University Libraries, and to Ohio State. Tracey shared some of her research interests related to Black youth, incarceration, rehabilitation, and recidivism. Prior to coming to Ohio State, Tracey worked at the Cleveland Public Library system as a paraprofessional for five years and then became a professional youth and educational librarian, serving in that role for 10 years. As a public librarian, Tracey developed programming related to science, technology, engineering, and math (STEM) to expose marginalized students to these career options, hands-on experiments, and a chance to meet real-life scientists who looked a lot like the youth who participated in the library STEM programming. Tracey cotaught extensive courses on General Education Development (GED) with Mr. Elliot Huff to ex-offenders and other underserved patrons wanting to pursue their education. Like many Black students interviewed in this study, Tracey, being a Black woman and a librarian within a predominantly White profession, has experienced discrimination, has worked doubly hard to make an impact within the communities she has served, and has been overlooked for professional leadership positions. What has kept Tracey going within the profession is a commitment to bringing awareness of information literacy to communities that are marginalized and advocating for equity, diversity, and inclusion in our profession.

During this conversation, Amanda brought up some of the questions that she had been wrestling with after attending the panel to see if Tracey might be interested in working together on a research study. As a White woman, Amanda knew that she did not have the lived experiences or perspectives to do a study like this responsibly on her own. However, she did have the research training and experience to help in the design and analysis processes. Tracey has the lived experience of being a Black woman in the United States, as well as experience with living, working, and servicing the Black and African American populations as a Black librarian, and she brings these experiences and perspectives to the study. As an untenured Black librarian, Tracey knew that there was a lot at stake for her to participate in such a study. Would her predominantly White, tenured colleagues find this to be a provocative or controversial study, and how would this affect her when colleagues vote on her own tenure and promotion case in a few years? After taking some time to think about it and speaking to tenured colleagues whom she trusted, Tracey felt comfortable moving forward, and we designed a study that explores Black and African American college students' experiences with libraries before and during college. This study forms the basis of this report. As we discuss in our companion report, *Narratives of (Dis) Enfranchisement: Reckoning with the History of Libraries and the Black and African American Experience*, research and scholarship about Black and African American library users are largely absent from the library and information science (LIS) literature, despite our profession's declared values related to equity, diversity, inclusivity, and social justice.

RACE AND THE LIS PROFESSION

The LIS profession is overwhelmingly White, and current statistics indicate that the overall demographics of the profession are not shifting toward diversity. According to 2010 ALA Counts data, 88 percent of librarians were White, even though White people made up only 63 percent of the US population around the same time (Bourg, 2014). At that same time, only 5 percent of librarians were Black or African American. More recent demographic data indicates that this percentage has remained static (Department for Professional Employees, 2020; Rosa & Henke, 2017), and recent statistics about library school enrollment indicate that it will continue to remain static (ALISE, 2020).

One may wonder why the demographics of the profession matter if LIS professionals have made a commitment to serve their diverse user communities. Although this commitment might be genuine, many White librarians are likely unaware of their own implicit and learned biases, as well as the ways in which race affects the daily lives of BIPOC, and may not feel the need to acknowledge or address the legacies of our profession's historical racial exclusion. Many White people in the United States currently take a color-blind or color-evasive approach to race, meaning that they think it is better (or more polite or comfortable) to avoid acknowledging race (Annamma et al., 2017; Bonilla-Silva, 2018; Burke, 2019). This approach might be deployed with good intentions, but it ends up maintaining White supremacy and toxicity in the long term. A color-evasive ideology is one that espouses the belief that race is no longer relevant to understanding society or that it is somehow racist to be aware of and acknowledge race. This latter point may even seem virtuous, in that one may believe that choosing not to acknowledge race somehow results in equality. However, the reason why color-evasive ideologies are harmful is that they often serve as "an assertion of equal opportunity that minimizes the reality of racism in favor of individual or cultural explanations of reality" (Burke, 2019, p. 2). In other words, they deny both the racialized experiences that BIPOC have with prejudiced individuals as well as the very existence of systemic racism, shifting the blame to BIPOC for perceived (and inaccurate) cultural deficits.

Many have argued that the LIS profession has indeed taken a color-evasive or race-neutral approach.

Tracie D. Hall (2012), who is the current executive director of the American Library Association, once wrote, "the library and information science field has seemingly slapped itself with a gag order [about race and racism]. While the discussion of diversity in libraries has proliferated over the past few decades, meaningful dialogue around race has been eviscerated or altogether evaded" (p. 198). Instead, the profession has focused more broadly on diversity and multiculturalism (Hudson, 2017; Pawley, 2006). Diversity and multiculturalism are important, but focusing just on these will not move the profession toward inclusivity, equity, and justice.

Although some research explores the experiences of Black and African American library users, as discussed in *Narratives of (Dis)Enfranchisement*, there is a lack of research that explores how race affects their experiences in libraries. This is critical given the overwhelming Whiteness of librarianship previously discussed. BIPOC experience racism and discrimination on a regular and frequent basis as they attempt to live their lives. We have no reason to believe that when BIPOC users pass through the doors of our buildings or enter our virtual spaces that they suddenly enter a race-neutral zone. Furthermore, BIPOC users do not shed their racialized identities when they are in our spaces; they bring their whole selves to the library, including the racism and discrimination that they experience with regularity in nonlibrary spaces. We cannot expect that they perceive a White person at the reference or circulation desk differently because they are in a library space. Because we do not have a basic understanding of how race affects library users' experiences, our profession is maintaining White supremacy while also espousing values related to diversity, inclusivity, equity, and social justice. The late Maya Angelou once said, "Do the best you can until you know better. Then when you know better, do better." We hope that this special report provides an opportunity for our profession to know better and do better by our BIPOC users, colleagues, and communities.

CHANGING THE NARRATIVE

In the chapters that follow, we dive into the library experiences that the 15 Black and African American students who participated in our study shared with us. In *Narratives of (Dis)Enfranchisement*, we contextualized these experiences by describing the racialized histories of our institutions, as well as the contemporary legacies of that history. In designing this study and conducting research for this book, we were disturbed at the exclusion of Black and African American library users' voices from our profession's literature. Until relatively recently, very little contemporary research or scholarship has focused specifically on the library experiences of this user population. Given the race-evasive nature of our profession, perhaps this should not be surprising. If we are truly committed to serving the Black and African American users who come through our doors, we must explore their experiences with libraries, including their needs and expectations. Although a single exploratory study such as this one cannot accomplish this task fully, we believe it is a start.

Critical race theory (CRT) did not explicitly inform the design of our study, but we believe that this study is aligned with CRT. CRT provides a theoretical foundation for exploring the ways in which BIPOC experience oppression while also considering other facets of their identity (e.g., gender, socioeconomic status, (dis)ability, etc.). Although scholars have articulated the core tenets of CRT in various ways, some of the commonly identified tenets include the acknowledgment that race and racism play central roles in the daily lives of BIPOC, the fact that color-evasive ideologies maintain the status quo, and the importance of counternarratives that elevate and honor the voices and lived experiences of BIPOC in moving toward a more just society. In particular, we intend for our study to elevate the voices and experiences of library users from whom we rarely hear. We hope that this study will be a conversation starter for considering how we can ensure that we are providing equitable and welcoming environments for our Black and African American library users, as well as meeting their needs and expectations.

Some of our White readers might find themselves feeling angry, frustrated, defensive, guilty, or upset when reading particular portions of this report and might be tempted to stop reading. It is possible that you have already experienced these emotions reading this introduction. We encourage you to take a moment to identify what caused the reaction or emotion, temporarily set it aside, continue reading, and then return to that reaction or emotion for some reflection. These feelings are part of a normal reaction to feeling racial discomfort (Tatum, 2017). Our goal is to be direct about how racism manifests in our libraries, schools, universities, and society. That is a difficult pill for many White people to swallow, especially when dominant narratives about race falsely state that racism is a thing of the past and that current disparities in economic status or educational outcomes are a result of deficient cultural values rather than race (Bonilla-Silva, 2018). If you are a White colleague, we hope that you are reading this book because you are committed to being antiracist, both personally and professionally. If you are in the early stages of this journey, please know that being uncomfortable is part of this journey, as antiracist work forces one to consider one's own role in maintaining the oppression of BIPOC.

STRUCTURE OF THIS REPORT

In the chapters that follow, we share the library experiences of the 15 Black and African American undergraduate students who participated in our study. Immediately following this introduction is a short chapter that describes our study, including how it was designed and how we collected and analyzed data. We then dedicate one chapter each to the students' experiences with public, school (K–12), and academic libraries. Before concluding, we take an in-depth look at the role(s) race played in the students' library experiences, including both the positive and the negative. In the final chapter, we offer reflections and recommendations for our White library peers, such as guidance for developing an antiracist mindset and more equitable service provision.

NOTE

1. At the time, Mr. Cornute was the program coordinator for the Todd Anthony Bell National Resource Center on the African American Male in the Office of Diversity and Inclusion at The Ohio State University. Dr. Travers was the graduate administrative associate at the Student Life Multicultural Center and a doctoral student in the Higher Education and Student Affairs program at The Ohio State University. He has since completed his doctoral work and earned his PhD.

2

ABOUT THIS STUDY

In this study, we explore the library experiences, both before and during college, of Black and African American students attending The Ohio State University, a predominantly White institution (PWI) in the Midwest. The following research questions formed the foundation for this study:

- How do Black and African American students describe their experiences with libraries and library staff, both before and during college?
- What role or purpose do Black and African American students assign to the libraries and library staff on their campus?
- Do prior experiences with libraries seem to inform college library usage for Black and African American students?

We recruited 15 undergraduate students who self-identified as Black and/or African American using personal connections in our institution's Office of Diversity and Inclusion and through snowball sampling (i.e., students who participated passed along information about the study to friends who they thought might be interested in participating). The students received a $15 Target gift card for completing a semistructured interview lasting no more than 60 minutes with one or both of the authors.

A question that we have regularly been asked when we have presented on this topic is, "Did you consider interviewing White students?" The answer is no. Typically the inquirer presses on, indicating that we cannot truly make statements about Black and African American users' experiences unless we compare them to those of White students. This is false. Following that approach, White library users are categorized as the normative reference group and Black and African American library users are considered to be the exception to that norm—aberrant, deviant, abnormal. It is possible to understand the experiences of marginalized populations without constant reference to the dominant population. In addition, the majority of LIS research has not accounted for race by disaggregating data. Sometimes this makes sense if the samples are too small for meaningful analysis, such as in inferential analysis. However, this also means that most LIS research is likely representative of White library users' perspectives or experiences. We do not lack LIS research exploring the usage and experiences of White library users, but we have a massive and glaring gap in scholarship exploring those topics related to BIPOC library users. Building on the historical legacy of Black and African American communities' experiences with libraries discussed in *Narratives of (Dis)Enfranchisement*, this report attempts to narrow that gap and provide a foundation for future research exploring the library experiences of BIPOC users.

METHODS

Phenomenology implicitly guided the design of this study. As a research methodology, the purpose of phenomenology is to explore, describe, and make sense of peoples' experiences with a particular phenomenon (van Manen, 1990). As such, the phenomenological question asks what it is like to experience a particular phenomenon, such as completing research assignments in college or interacting with librarians and library staff. It is critical for the researcher to collect rich data related to the participants' experiences to describe, to the fullest extent possible, experiences with the phenomenon. The researcher will make interpretations about the nature of these experiences based on their own experiences and existing scholarship, so it can be useful to provide the participants with the opportunity to reflect upon and interpret their experiences with the phenomenon during the data collection phase.

Data Collection

We used Seidman's (2013) approach to phenomenological interviewing to develop the semi-structured interview protocol used to collect data, as it provides researchers with a method to collect rich data related to the participants' experiences of a phenomenon and their interpretations of their experiences. Seidman notes that the purpose of phenomenological interviewing is to understand "the lived experience of other people and the meaning they make of that experience" (Seidman, 2013, p. 9). To do this, Seidman recommends a three-interview series that includes a "focused life history," "details of the experience," and "reflection on meaning." In general, this three-interview series collects details about participants' past and present lived experiences with the phenomenon, as well as asking them to reflect

on the meaning of these lived experiences, including both their "intellectual and emotional connections" (Seidman, 2013, p. 22). Seidman recommends that each interview last approximately 90 minutes and that the interviews be spaced several days apart. Although researchers can modify the structure of the interview series, he does encourage researchers to respect the structure. However, he notes that researchers need to consider what is "rational . . . repeatable and documentable" (Seidman, 2013, p. 25). Researchers must consider the availability of resources, including both in time and in money, as well as the size of the sample desired to develop nuanced interpretation of the phenomenon being studied. For this research study, conducting three 90-minute interviews with each participant simply would not have been feasible given the diversity of experiences that we were trying to collect. Therefore, we used Seidman's three-interview series to develop a single semistructured interview protocol.

The semistructured interview protocol was divided into four sections based on Seidman's (2013) approach. First, to get students comfortable talking about themselves and to learn a little more about them, we asked questions related to their backgrounds (e.g., their year, major(s), hometown, etc.) as well as initial thoughts about librarians and libraries. We asked them what words come to mind when they think of libraries and to picture a librarian in their minds and describe that picture to us. The second section asked the students to describe their experiences with libraries and interactions with librarians[1] before college, which mostly focused on experiences in public and school libraries. In the third section, we asked students about their experiences with libraries and interactions with librarians in college and about the differences between research assignments and expectations in high school versus college. Finally, we asked students to reflect on the role of race in their experiences in libraries and interactions with librarians. If the student was comfortable with our doing so, we also probed a little more deeply by asking about their mental depiction of librarians and what role, if any, race may have played in their engagement with librarians.

As mentioned previously, the students who participated may have been interviewed by one or both of us, the researchers. This is potentially an important limitation to the study, as Amanda, a White woman, participated in eight interviews, four by herself and four with Tracey. This may have affected the students' responses to questions, particularly questions related to race. Amanda had no established relationships with these students prior to the interviews, so they may not have felt as comfortable discussing issues of race with her as they would have with a BIPOC interviewer or someone with whom they had already established a trusting relationship. If we were to do this study again, we would have a BIPOC librarian or researcher conduct all of the interviews. Despite this, we still believe we have collected rich data that is of value to the profession. We hope that after reading the subsequent chapters you will agree.

Data Analysis
With the students' consent,[2] the interviews were audio recorded and then sent to a professional service for transcription. The authors collaboratively developed a coding schema based on the interview protocols and emergent themes. We coded approximately three transcripts together using Dedoose (https://www.dedoose.com/), a web-based qualitative analysis tool, to ensure that we were applying the codes consistently, and this provided the opportunity to identify new codes. After that, we each coded the remaining transcripts individually, and those codes were also entered into Dedoose to facilitate analysis.

OUR PARTICIPANTS
Despite using a combination of convenience and snowball sampling, we were able to recruit a diverse group of students to participate in our study. Table 2.1 provides an alphabetical listing of the students' pseudonyms as well as some basic demographic information about each student. As shown, the students who participated represented a variety of majors and were at different points in their collegiate careers. Even though Ohio State is one of the largest universities in the United States, some of the students' major fields of

TABLE 2.1
Student Profiles

PSEUDONYM	YEAR	MAJOR (GENERAL)	GENDER
Camaron	Third	Biological and Health Sciences	Male
Chloe	Second	Arts and Architecture	Female
Darius	Third	Biological and Health Sciences	Male
Destiny	Third	Behavioral and Social Sciences	Female
Diamond	Second	Behavioral and Social Sciences	Female
Elijah	Third	Engineering and Physical Sciences	Male
Imani	Third	Behavioral and Social Sciences	Female
Isis	Second	Business and Management	Female
Jada	First	Business and Management	Female
Jasmine	Third	Biological and Health Sciences	Female
Jaylen	Third	Engineering and Physical Sciences	Male
Malik	First	Business and Management	Male
Sekhmet	Fourth	Biological and Health Sciences	Female
Tahuti	Second	Arts and Architecture	Male
Trinity	Second	Behavioral and Social Sciences	Female

TABLE 2.2
Students' On-Campus Involvement

ORGANIZATIONS	ACTIVITIES AND PROGRAMS
African Youth League	African American Voices Gospel Choir
Alpha Phi Alpha	Bell National Resource Center
Black Mental Health Coalition	Buck-I-Serv
Black Student Association	Stadium Scholars
Eritrean and Ethiopian Student Association	Taste of Columbus
NAACP Young Scholars Program	
National Society of Black Engineers	
Natural and Prosperous Society	

study are quite small and it is possible that a student was the only Black or African American student in a particular major. To maintain confidentiality, we have decided not to share their specific majors. Some of the students had double majors or had a minor(s). Four of the fifteen students, three female students and one male student, were also library student employees. To protect their identities, we have not identified them here, and we also protect their identities when using any quotations from them about their experiences as student employees.

Not surprisingly, the students who participated in the study are high achievers and were engaged with campus activities. Table 2.2 identifies some of the activities and organizations the students were active in, and in many cases, the students held leadership positions.

LIMITATIONS

This study was designed to be exploratory in nature, and we have assembled a robust sample to accomplish that initial goal. We knew that the experiences, stories, and perspectives that our participants would share with us would be interesting and rich. We intended to identify aspects of these students' experiences that warranted further research. When we initiated this work, writing a book was not on our minds. Therefore, in reading what follows, it is important

to know that these experiences and perspectives are representative of the sample of participants in this study, many of whom grew up and continued to live in the same geographical region in the Midwest and who all attend a very large research university that is predominantly White and are of what is typically considered traditional college-going age (i.e., 18 to 24 years old). Further research that includes students from different regions of the country attending different kinds of institutions and with different college-going experiences is absolutely necessary to gain a more complete portrait of Black and African American students' experiences with libraries. In addition, many of the topics that we cover in this book really just skim the surface and are likely the tip of a deep iceberg.

NOTES

1. In the interviews, we did not ask students to make a distinction between librarians and paraprofessional library staff, as those kinds of distinctions are often invisible or unimportant to users. From our perspective, we were more interested in learning about whether their interactions with library staff were welcoming or alienating and in attempting to understand how those interactions might shape future library use. Throughout this special report we use the terms librarian and library staff interchangeably.

2. This study was determined to be exempt by The Ohio State University's Institutional Review Board.

3
PUBLIC LIBRARIES

In this chapter, we share the students' experiences with public libraries. A common theme among the students in our study is that they were either regular or frequent users of their public libraries. For many of the students, their initial encounters with the library were with a family member, but they reported transitioning to going to the library to get their own reading materials. Their public library usage changed over time, however, even for those who still reported using their public libraries as college students. Many of the students self-identified as "big readers" when they were children, but this identity seemed to change as they got older and faced increased academic and social demands. Finally, students reported various experiences in engaging with public library staff, ranging from supportive relationships to friendly and helpful transactions to almost no interaction at all.

THE IMPORTANCE OF FAMILY

Prior to high school, family members were integral to the students' introduction to and continued engagement with public libraries. Thirteen of the fifteen students spoke about family in connection to their public library use. In particular, students spoke about the ways in which their mothers and their siblings shaped their library experiences.

Most of the students who discussed family indicated that their parents, particularly their mothers, had introduced them to the library. The context for the introduction varied, but several different themes emerged. For a few students, their mothers were regular library users, and the student would visit the library with her when she went to get her books, attend programming, or use the computers. In other cases, students were aware that their parents took them to the library for various kinds of enrichment, such as getting books to read or participating in programming, especially summer reading programs. For example, Sekhmet shared,

> Even during the summer when I wouldn't have school, my mom would drop me off at a library every day, a different one, and I would get like twenty books, finish them in the day, go to the next library, return them, and start again.

In this example, Sekhmet's mother is implicitly supporting her daughter's enrichment by taking her to different libraries on a daily basis to get new books to read. In other cases, the students indicated that their parents had explicitly expressed their desire to help develop their reading and intellectual abilities. Imani indicated that her mother took Imani and her sister to the library to "progress our reading abilities." Diamond shared that her father used to "force" her to go to the public library and participate in the summer reading program. She elaborated, "He wanted me to get books for myself. . . . He was trying to basically encourage me and motivate me to read, starting from a really young age." When asked if this was because he enjoyed reading, Diamond explained,

> No . . . actually he didn't finish high school or college, because he grew up in Ethiopia, and at that time there wasn't a lot of political stability. So he was always big on education and . . . the experience that he has had in the past was the reason why he motivated me and my sisters to read all the time, do good in school, educate ourselves.

Darius's grandmother, who was "big on reading," also perceived the importance of library use for Darius and his siblings, with Darius noting that she would offer to take them to the library or call up his family members and tell them to take Darius and his siblings to the library.

Many of the students indicated that when they were children, they would often visit the library with their siblings. Sometimes they went as a family (i.e., with their parent[s]), and other times they were able to go to the library without their parents. Destiny said that she and her sister would go to the library with their mother so she could use the internet. Destiny and her sister used that time to find comic books to read. Before Jaylen and his siblings got into sports, they would go to the library every day after school to do their homework, and their parents would come pick them up at closing time. Jasmine shared, "Especially during the summer, me, my sister, we'd just go to the library, find books to read, and . . . walk down [to the library]." Many students recalled these memories somewhat unemotionally, just as a matter of fact. However, when other students described the time they shared at the library with their siblings, it was clear that it was a time during which they bonded and

developed some camaraderie. For example, Jasmine and her sister teamed up to find books in series they enjoyed. She shared,

> Me and my sister, we'd always kind of know what books we wanted to read. Like we would read a lot of books in a series, so it's like you finish this one, you know which one you want to read next.

As will be shared in an upcoming section, some of these siblings used to develop reading competitions with each other.

A couple of students reported that their family members served as a form of social capital for them when they visited the library. Although this did not emerge as a significant theme across all 15 interviews, we think this is important to include due to the discrimination that many of the students reported facing, particularly at public libraries in predominantly White neighborhoods. Imani recalled that once when she was using a public library in a predominantly White neighborhood as a child, she asked library staff for help when she was looking for books. The librarians were not helpful, so she asked her mother instead:

> And my mom would take it into her own hands, and she would lead me to the shelf and help me find what I was looking for. So I think my mom was actually more helpful than the person on staff.

Camaron, on the other hand, went to his local public library, also in a predominantly White neighborhood, with his younger sister when he was home from college for a visit. He never developed a relationship with the staff at the library, but he indicated that his sister knew the staff there. "And she would actually go up and talk to the guy who works at the desk, just because she's there like all the time and they know each other." He indicated that it never occurred to him to talk to the library staff, even if he needed something. Though he did not explicitly say this could be due to how White library staff might potentially react to him, an African American male, other male students in our study indicated that they were aware that they could be viewed as more threatening or dangerous than other patrons in the library, which is discussed in more depth in chapter 6.

LIBRARY USE

As mentioned previously, most of the students in the study reported being regular, if not frequent, users of their public libraries, especially prior to college. Some students used the same library location throughout their precollege years, and others reported going to multiple locations. In the previous section, we discussed how important family was to these students' public library experiences. Other than visiting libraries with family members, typically mothers or siblings, public library usage was primarily an individual activity for these students. Going to the library was not a social activity for these students, with one notable exception: Isis. She grew up in a lower-income neighborhood in a regional city, and the neighborhood library became a refuge for kids who wanted to have fun but stay out of trouble. She reflected that visiting the library

> was an outlet to stay out of trouble. A lot of our friends were doing what they weren't supposed to be doing. We spent time in the library, whether it was [using the] computer, reading . . . so it was kind of like the center of my neighborhood and kind of like an alternative to some of the things, some of the bad things, that were going on in my neighborhood.

Isis was not the only one of her peers to find refuge in the neighborhood library. She noted that sometimes so many kids would come that it would start to get loud and the staff would have to ask some of them to leave.

As one might expect, the students reported using public libraries to check out reading materials and movies, to use the computers, and to support their academic pursuits. Computer usage included playing video games as well as finding resources for their school assignments. Especially as the students got older, they began to see the public library as a quiet place to study and work, and several students reported going to the library to study for the SAT or ACT, to complete college applications, and to fill out applications for scholarships and financial aid. For the most part, the students in the study did not report participating in programming other than summer reading programs at their public libraries.

Attitudes toward Reading

Most of the students in the study shared that they had loved to read when they were younger, often describing their younger selves as "big readers." This identity as a big reader was strongly connected to students' public library use, especially as children.[1] In addition to regularly going to their public libraries to get reading materials, many students reported participating in their libraries' summer reading programs.

Although most students reported being big readers, for some students this identity formed over time. For example, Trinity and her siblings often did not want to go with their mother to the library when they were young and would complain about it, asking, "Mom, we have to go again?" However, she noted that her attitude changed when she was about 10 years old, sharing that she started "reading everything off the shelves . . . and that was such an amazing thing, because it's free information." Diamond also alluded to an evolution in her feelings about reading, saying that she began to read regularly once she realized that she really liked to read, and it was no longer something she did because her father wanted her to. Isis, on the other hand, seemed to always feel positive about reading, but her relationship with reading deepened over time. She shared,

> Reading, as time progressed . . . became like my best friend. It'd keep me company when I was bored, when my mind was not in the right places, so, yeah, I spent pretty much every day that I could there [in the public library].

Isis's love of reading was modeled by her mother, and this was the case for about half of the students in the study—they had parents who liked to read, and as they grew up, they inherited this trait. Isis said she would question her mother, "Mom, who gets excited about books?" while realizing that "on the inside, I knew I was excited too." Darius shared that his parents are historians and his father writes books, so he would observe them in the process of reading and writing for their professional pursuits. This observation encouraged him to read from a young age, and his parents would nurture this interest by taking him to the library or buying him books.

In addition to observing parents reading for pleasure or for professional pursuits, there were a few different motivations for reading that the students shared. Many seemed to enjoy reading simply for reading's sake when they were younger. For example, Jaylen mentioned that he "found a lot of joy in books" because he could really get into them. The students reported regularly checking out a steady stream of books from the library, only occasionally highlighting their love of particular series, such as Magic Tree House or Harry Potter. Most of the students just seemed to want to read as much as they possibly could. Some students read to learn more about specific interests that they had. Jaylen really got into reading historical fiction, which led to him seeking out books on African American figures. Camaron, who liked sports, said,

> When I was a kid, I would always go to the sports sections. And I would go to see if they had any Matt Christopher books, because I like the stories that he wrote. . . . and I would read the sports almanacs and just learn everything about a year in sports that happened in like the NBA. I read a lot of biographies about certain players and stuff.

When the students were reading for reading's sake or had specific interests, there was definitely a desire to learn that was evident in their reflections. Jada expressed gratitude that her mother encouraged and supported her reading interests as a child, stating "I feel like that [reading and going to the library] helped a lot because reading a lot makes you learn."

Many students reported channeling their love of reading through summer reading programs and some really enjoyed the competition that these programs brought, as well as the rewards they received for their achievements. Diamond shared, "I loved getting prizes. I liked the competition." Diamond was one of the handful of students who reported creating reading competitions with their siblings. She reflected,

> The summer after fourth grade, we had a competition of who can read the fastest. . . . And we read the Harry Potter series. And we actually fell in love with the series. It was crazy. Like we woke up early in the morning, read it all day, and then we would finish. And those books are really thick. So we'd finish each book within like three days, because we were just addicted to it.

Jada reported doing something similar with her sisters.

> We would kind of make it a competition as far as reading books. We would be like, "Oh, I have this book to read. I bet you can't finish this one before me." And it would be totally different books, different pages, and everything.

She said that they would drive their mother crazy because they were finishing books so quickly and would ask to go back to the library to get more. Even though these students and their siblings set this up as a competition, it was clearly a way in which they bonded over a shared interest and also something they remembered fondly.

Most students reported a change in their reading habits as they got older, however. Although some students remained big readers, there seemed to be a shift as students moved on to middle school and high school. Diamond reflected, "I got my first phone in eighth grade, so after that, once I got on social media, I started to read a lot less." Darius seemed to indicate that his identity as a big reader did not persist as he got older, that it was mostly associated with his younger self, saying, "Yeah, definitely as a kid." Some students seemed to share a nostalgia for their former reading habits. For example, Jasmine reflected, "Yeah, I used to like really love to read. I wish I still continued to read." Diamond shared a similar sentiment, stating, "I still love reading, but I don't do it that often, unfortunately. Which I'm trying to get back to doing more."

The students also spoke about how the demands of college affected their leisure-reading habits, especially because there is so much required reading in their college courses. Jada shared that the reading load in her English course is heavy. She tells her sister,

> You should see what I have to read in college. . . . You think you like reading now, wait until you get to college. . . . It's reading, but it's just certain stuff in college, it's just so boring. . . . I feel like some of the stuff we read, it's just like, "Why are we reading this?" But, I mean, we're supposed to learn.

Other students spoke about having limited time to fit leisure reading into their busy schedules. Darius remarked, "You really don't have much free time, you know."

However, many students reported a desire to continue reading, as well as their strategies for continuing to read for leisure as much as they possibly could. A few students spoke about how their collegiate academic lives helped them to do this. Jada expressed some skepticism about the common read for her first year in college, sharing that her initial reaction was, "Really? Do I have to read this book before college?" After she started reading, she felt differently about it. "Once I started to read it, I was like 'Oh, this is nice.' And I couldn't stop reading it after that." Elijah used his elective courses to help fulfill his desire to read, because he realized he wasn't reading a lot of books that weren't assigned to him in his courses. Being a STEM student, he wanted courses that were "something other than math or numbers" and that required him to read books that he finds "intellectually stimulating."

Perhaps not surprisingly, many students reported using their winter and summer breaks to reconnect with their leisure-reading habits, even if they reported being busy with schoolwork, employment, or internships. Elijah shared,

> Over the summer, I definitely tried to read one or two books when I had no homework. . . . I still had an internship, so I still had other responsibilities, but I did read a little bit. I was really proud of that, and I hope that's something I can continue to do, once I'm not doing things 24/7.

Darius also reported finding time for leisure reading during his breaks: "I try to make myself—especially during summer break, I always try to make myself read at least a book a month, or something like that." Isis said, "I'll go home for break . . . and I'll go walk over to the library and get a new book, and I'll read it over break. You know, just to keep my brain going." Even though these students reported a desire to read for leisure and spoke about their childhood reading habits in a nostalgic manner, many had to prioritize finding the time to feed that desire when they got older.

Changes in Public Library Use over Time

Similar to the changes in reading habits as they got older that students shared, the ways in which they used public libraries also changed over time. It is impossible to determine causation, but there does seem to be a relationship between students' public library use and their leisure-reading habits. What appears to have remained consistent is the perception that libraries are for learning. When these students were kids, learning might have included learning to read or learning to love to read, and as they got older, they used the library to focus on their schoolwork and academic endeavors.

Many students noted that as they got older, they came to appreciate that the library was a quiet place in which they could study or be productive academically. Jasmine shared, "In high school, I mostly [used the public library for] studying for the ACT and then work on college applications." She said that the library provided a "quiet space" where she wouldn't get "distracted," especially by her younger siblings and other family members. Elijah described the shift in use of the library as he completed high school and began to think about attending college:

I took a gap year after I graduated [high school], and I spent a lot of time in libraries there. . . . I had a lot of free time. I would go read books all the time, and then I had to take the SAT and ACT. . . . I would go and study and practice and stuff like that. I think, kind of from then on, it was more about . . . going to do something . . . and this is a place where I can be efficient and do things and get things done.

In addition to using the public library to study for his ACT and SAT, Camaron continued to use his public library when he went back home to visit. "I do have some nice public libraries around where I'm from, so I'd use those. And I actually still, whenever I go back home, I would use up some time studying for something [at the public library]." He highlighted that the library was conveniently located and provided him with a "quiet environment" in which he could be productive.

Although many of the students continued to use public libraries throughout high school and college, their library use shifted from a place to find reading materials to a space in which they could concentrate and study. Again, the common theme is that public libraries were spaces dedicated to learning. Jasmine summed this up nicely:

When I went back [to my public library], it was like I hadn't gone in a little bit. And it was sort of funny to do my [organic chemistry homework] and then there's all these kids around learning how to read.

(DIS)ENGAGEMENT WITH LIBRARY STAFF

With the exception of reading program participation, the students, for the most part, did not spontaneously discuss interactions or engagement with public library staff. Given the purpose of the study, this is something we were interested in, so we asked specific questions to learn more about the students' interactions with staff in public libraries. We found that many students did have interactions with public library staff, some positive and some negative, though only a couple of students experienced true engagement. Despite these

interactions, at least half the students indicated that library staff did not actively promote programming or materials to them. Most of these students were unaware that public libraries might offer programming beyond summer reading programs.

A few students indicated that the majority of their interactions with public library staff were transactional in nature, such as checking out materials. Jasmine indicated that she never really felt the need to interact with the library staff because she and her sister mostly knew what they wanted to read next. Even though Jasmine reported that they were in the library all the time when they were kids and she believed the staff did recognize them, no one initiated interactions related to readers' advisory service or programming with them. As she got older, the only interaction she had was asking staff for the Wi-Fi code. Elijah had a similar experience to young Jasmine, in that his frequent library usage resulted in the staff recognizing him, but the interactions never went beyond a head nod and perhaps a hello.

Several students shared interactions that went a step further than basic transactions and spoke about how they reached out to library staff for help. Many of these students reported positive outcomes; for example, Diamond shared, "If I wanted to find a book and I needed help picking a book, I would ask a librarian and they would suggest ideas based off of my past books that I've read, which was helpful." A few students, however, shared negative experiences with asking a public library staff member for assistance, and the response received could vary among the staff members. Malik reported that once when he had asked for help, the staff member got up and showed him where the books were. Although the example he gave in the interview was an older white male, he felt that many white librarians were "standbackish" with him. He elaborated, "They interacted somewhat, but it was like they were kind of standbackish. But if you asked them something, they would help and accommodate." Though she did not attribute her specific example to racial differences,[2] Sekhmet also shared varying responses from library staff when she approached them. She explained,

The librarians I've mostly been talking about have been the children's librarians. They've been wonderful. They actually care about the kids. As you get older and you go into the more adult ones, adult librarians, they tend to be the more coarse ones. They're not very engaging and if they don't like you, they will still help you but they will not put their all into helping you. . . . It's like once you start high school, after that it's just downhill for you if you go to an adult librarian. . . . When I was little and I had to go ask a question to the adult librarian, there wasn't a connection. There's just like a, "What do you want? What do you need? Okay, get out of my way."

Imani shared a similar experience of when she had approached a library staff member for help as a child:

Sometimes they weren't helpful. I remember often going back to my mom, like, "Oh, the librarian says she can't do this, this, or other." And my mom would take it into her own hands and she would lead me to the shelf and help me find what I was looking for. So I think my mom was actually more helpful than the person on staff."

Another student, Tahuti, indicated that his experiences interacting with public library staff depended on which branch he was using. He reported having more positive experiences with staff at the urban branches that served diverse neighborhoods and negative experiences at suburban branches serving predominantly White neighborhoods. He shared,

I would say that at the [urban branch], they were more positive in having the African American community together. They taught me about tutoring options at the [different urban branch]. But the more suburban ones, they were kind of, you checked a book out. . . . If you had any questions, they would normally be engaging towards you. You had to kind of ask.

As he began to describe specific experiences, Tahuti's characterization of the staff at the suburban branches

changed a bit, and he ultimately felt like they were "dismissive" of him when he would reach out for help. Among the students in our study, Tahuti was not alone in feeling like library staff were indifferent to his needs due to racial differences. Because of the significance of this topic—the ways in which race has impacted these students' experiences with libraries—we have devoted chapter 6 to this issue and will not cover it in depth in this chapter.

Only a couple of students shared memories of what we consider to be true engagement with public library staff. By true engagement we mean that students developed a positive relationship with library staff, one that went beyond a transactional nature and basic help interactions. Both of the students whose experiences we believe exhibited true engagement interacted with library staff serving diverse neighborhoods. In addition, both of them worked in their libraries—one as a volunteer and the other as an intern. However, for both of these women, the relationships seemed to have been developed before they began an employee-like relationship with their libraries.[3] Although these students are outliers, we believe this indicates that their experiences with public library staff are noteworthy and worth sharing.

Jada was one of the two students who reported developing relationships with public library staff. Positive interactions with library staff began with basic help requests. She shared,

A lot of the librarians that I had interactions with, they were very helpful. They're willing to help you start making copies when I wanted to make copies. Helping me find a book if I needed a book. And then as far as the summer reading program, there were a lot of helpful staff members. . . . They help with homework.

Over time, the library staff got to know Jada by name, and she really appreciated when they would give her suggestions about what to read next.

I loved when they did that [readers' advisory], because it's like some people, they go in and they only read certain books. But then once they start telling me about other ones, [it was like] "Oh, I can read this one, and this one, and this one." So it was like I had a lot of options versus me just sticking to one type of genre. It was nice.

In high school, Jada participated in a career preparation program, which included a paid summer internship. The students were able to pick where they wanted to work, and Jada chose the local public library system because she believed it would help prepare her to study business at the university.

Isis was the other student who reported developing relationships with the staff at her public library. Isis's experience seemed to be similar to Jada's in that she was also a regular library user, participated in the summer reading program, the staff got to know her by name over time, and she also had an employment-like relationship with her library. Isis expressed a much deeper connection with her library than did any other student. As mentioned previously, Isis, who lived in a high-violence neighborhood in a regional city, described the library as a place of refuge for her and her friends, a place they could go to be safe and to stay out of trouble. She also discussed the significant role that reading played in her life and in her mother's life and the ways in which their love of reading really helped them to connect. The library staff also demonstrated an interest in her academic life, helping her to apply for scholarships and asking her how school was going, even after she began college. In addition to the contributions that she made as a volunteer, Isis had a special experience that really made her feel like both she and the library were making reciprocal investments in each other. Her public library branch worked with a well-known artist to re-create a mural of prominent African American figures, including Sojourner Truth, Frederick Douglass, Martin Luther King Jr., and Malcolm X, using broken up tiles, and Isis had the opportunity to participate in this project. Isis described this experience as "one of my huge contributions to that library," and the library staff helped to reinforce that belief. She reflected, "We had a huge ceremony in the front lawn. It was amazing. All the librarians came out and [it] was like, 'You helped with this?' I was like, 'You know I did.'" This re-created mural was a point of pride, not just for Isis or the library, but also for her community. Isis summarized her experiences with her public library by sharing, "I made really good connections with really good people."

CONCLUSION

Through the interviews, we learned that public libraries were clearly important to the students' families and played a significant role in their childhood, particularly in terms of nurturing their love of reading, offering access to materials, and providing a space for their academic endeavors. Given the historical fight for access to public libraries, which we discuss in chapter 3 of our companion special report, *Narratives of (Dis) Enfranchisement: Reckoning with the History of Libraries and the Black and African American Experience*, these findings are important. As Beasley (2017) powerfully wrote, the learning that libraries afforded to the Black and African American communities resulted in feelings of self-worth that could be channeled toward emancipation. Furthermore, we should not be surprised that family members were instrumental in the students' usage of the libraries for nurturing reading habits due to the generational trauma of forced illiteracy for Black Americans and African Americans in the United States (Duster, 2009). However, many of the specific authors or series that the students highlighted were White or White authored. As is discussed in chapter 4 of *(Dis)Enfranchisement*, many Black and African American children lack reading materials that include main characters who look like them or are written by Black and African American authors.

Several students intimated that their public libraries were a place of refuge for them. For example, Isis shared how the public library in her neighborhood quite literally kept her and her peers out of trouble by providing a safe space for them to go after school or on the weekends. For other students, the public library as refuge was less literal, less tangible. It provided a space for them to feed their desire to read and learn, as well as the opportunities for them to develop relationships with their siblings around their shared love of reading. However, several students shared how they did not necessarily feel comfortable in some public libraries, echoing treatment discussed in Agosto and Hughes-Hassell's (2005) study exploring the information-seeking behaviors of urban teenagers, the overwhelming majority of whom were African American, including library staff being dismissive toward them. The legacy of discrimination and exclusion is evident in the experiences that some of the students shared and is addressed in more depth in chapter 6.

Teen librarians and services for teens, including makerspaces and digital labs, were completely absent from the students' experiences. We did not specifically ask students about these topics, but they also did not come up organically as significant or meaningful experiences with their public libraries. Although the availability of these spaces and resources varies from library to library, many of these students were using large urban library systems in which these services are common. This absence echoes the perceptions of the students in Agosto and Hughes-Hassell's (2005) study in that there seemed to be a gap in services for teens. Many students spoke about children's librarians and adult librarians, but their library experiences seemed to be more solitary and academic in nature as they moved into their teen years. This might have implications for how these students used their academic libraries, as many of them did not know how librarians could support their learning in college, as is discussed in chapter 5. Although the findings of this study are not generalizable to all Black and African American teens, or even to those in just the state of Ohio, this absence should not be ignored. In 2015 the Young Adult Library Services Association (YALSA) noted that almost 50 percent of youth (ages 0 to 17) are BIPOC (YALSA, 2015). YALSA includes "cultural competency and responsiveness" as a core competency for teen librarians among other competencies that relate to engaging youth populations in various kinds of learning enrichment experiences (YALSA, 2017). Due to the changing demographics of American youth, YALSA has also highlighted empirical explorations of "equity of access" and "cultural competence, social justice and equity" in supporting teen populations in its National Research Agenda (YALSA, n.d.).

NOTES

1. This identity was also manifest in students' reflections on their experiences with their school libraries, particularly their elementary school experiences. Many students also reported participating in their elementary schools' reading challenges or competitions, which is discussed in chapter 4.

2. Sekhmet did report negative interactions with public library staff in her interview, which is covered in more depth in chapter 6.

3. As is discussed in chapter 5, library employment does not necessarily result in engagement. Several of the students in the study were library student employees at the university, and they were not necessarily more engaged with librarians and library staff than were the other students.

4
SCHOOL LIBRARIES

Although their experiences with public libraries were varied, all of the students could describe significant experiences with public libraries before college. However, their experiences with school libraries were even more varied, with some students describing significant experiences with elementary school libraries and others indicating not having high school libraries. A shift in how they used their school libraries, one similar to the shift in their public library usage, was also evident in their experiences as they transitioned from elementary school to high school.

ELEMENTARY SCHOOL

About half of the students shared experiences with their elementary school libraries or librarians. Most of these students equated elementary school libraries with reading, and for many of them, this was a positive association. Elijah shared fond memories of reading in his elementary school library, noting that it was his "favorite place." He said that the library had a bathtub full of cushions where students could read. "It was like a reading corner type thing, and I remember myself in there reading books, just being so happy to be in the little bathtub." Although Tahuti used the word *leisure* to describe his experiences with his elementary school library, he also shared that it was a place for his learning and growth. He had difficulty reading when he was young, and the librarian, in collaboration with his mother, would help him with his reading skills. Students also spoke with fondness about book fairs that were hosted in their libraries and reading challenges. Camaron and Destiny both spoke about how they liked the book fairs. Even though Destiny said she could not afford to buy books, she still enjoyed going to look through all the books and that it added a more fun component to an otherwise "boring" school day. Elijah and Jasmine both really enjoyed the reading challenges because they both loved to read and would often be top point scorers.

Of the students who shared their experiences with elementary school libraries, not all had such fond recollections. Many of the students shared that their classes regularly went to the library each day or each week for a period of time. Diamond said that she went to the elementary school library only because they were "required" to go each week. However, she said that they would read in the library and she found that to be "helpful." Destiny, on the hand, used stronger language, saying that they were "forced" to go every week. When asked about her use of language, she laughed and suggested that might have been a bit too strong of a word. She explained that when she would go to the public library or the college library where her mother was a student, she and her sister would play video games, which was fun. However, "with [elementary] school, we would have to speak all quiet and sit and read and it was not fun." Even though Destiny enjoyed going to libraries, including to read, she seemed to enjoy the experience more when she was doing this with her family.

Many of these students also shared their perceptions of or interactions with their elementary school librarians. Five of the six librarians whom the students discussed were perceived to be White women. Jada was the only student who shared that she had a librarian whom she believed to be Black or African American, but she did not share details about the librarian's personality and demeanor or their interactions. Tahuti, Elijah, and Camaron all spoke positively about their elementary school librarians. Elijah said that his librarian would "congratulate" you if you got your name on the board for the reading competition. Tahuti described his librarian as "sweet" and was appreciative of the time she spent with him helping him to improve his reading skills. Camaron said that he would go back to visit his elementary school librarian when he was in high school and "she was happy to see me." However, Destiny and Jaylen did not connect as well with their elementary school librarians. Destiny described her elementary school librarian as the stereotypical librarian, an "old lady" who shushed the students a lot. Jaylen also described his elementary school librarian as "older" and "stern," but he also said that she was "knowledgeable."

MIDDLE SCHOOL

Two-thirds of the students spoke about their middle school libraries or librarians, though often not in as much depth or detail as those who spoke about their elementary school libraries or librarians. The frequency of use that these students reported for their middle school libraries varied from student to student. Both Trinity and Destiny reported rarely using their middle school libraries. Destiny shared, "I don't think I stepped foot in it. I don't think I ever checked for the books."

Malik also reported rarely using his middle school library, opting to go to his public library instead. Other students, like Camaron and Isis, regularly visited their middle school libraries. Isis would regularly go to the library for her classes, during which she learned how to cite sources for her academic work. Camaron, on the other hand, voluntarily used the library, noting that the librarian was a family friend. He shared, "I'd say in middle school, if I wasn't going to the public library, I definitely was in the library . . . because I knew the librarian." Chloe was another student who rarely used her middle school library and did not appear to have engaged with her librarian, but she enjoyed going to the library for the book fairs. Jada spoke fondly of the author visits that her middle school library would host. She said that if you read the book, "it [the author visit] makes you understand the book and the author better, like why they wrote the book and what exactly their purpose of writing [the] book was." Trinity mentioned that her middle school librarian offered a book club, but it did not sound like she participated. She stated the book club was something that the librarian did not promote with the students, rather "it was something that students sought out for that resource." The librarian did not visit Trinity's classes, so she might not have felt comfortable joining the book club without an existing relationship.

Several students spoke about their middle school librarians and their interactions with them, which, similar to their usage of their middle school libraries, varied. Destiny was not sure if her middle school had a librarian. She said, "I don't remember any librarian. I'm sure there was one, but they never interacted with us." She shared that she recently learned, due to her student employment in her university's library, that librarians do more than sit at a desk, that being a librarian requires education. She added, "I don't know if there was a person who was officially a librarian or if it was just someone who worked the desk because they were understaffed. It could be either way." Other students mentioned that they knew they had a librarian in middle school but did not elaborate much on their experiences or interactions with that librarian. For example, when asked to picture a librarian in her head and describe that person to us, Jasmine described her middle school librarian. "She's there to help you out. Like find books or something. I mostly think of like middle school."

Other students had more frequent interactions with their librarians and developed relationships with them. Jaylen, for example, shared that he would visit his middle school and high school librarians when he went home to visit, something he said he would not have done with his public librarians. Despite this, he did not share many details about what fostered these lasting relationships with these librarians. Isis shared quite a bit of detail about her middle school librarian, Miss Washington (pseudonym). She said that Miss Washington was "tough" and had "strict rules." She would occasionally embarrass students if she deemed their behavior to be inappropriate (e.g., chewing gum in the library). Despite this, Isis seemed to express understanding if not appreciation toward Miss Washington. She reflected,

> She was tough, but I can see why. Her discipline was kind of like a shocker at first, but then, after a while, you [were] kind of like, "Okay, I understand why she did what she did." . . . She kind of had this motherly thing going on. She just had zero tolerance for certain behaviors.

Isis shared that the students would engage in friendly banter with Miss Washington about their fashion choices, indicating that Miss Washington seemed to connect with her students even if she was strict with them. Although not all of the students who spoke about their middle school librarians disclosed the perceived race of the librarians, Miss Washington was the only Black or African American middle school librarian that we know of in the study.

The beginning of the shift in how students perceived the purpose of libraries or the role that libraries could and should play in their lives is evident in some of what these students shared about their middle school library experiences. Jada said, "I didn't really read a lot of books from that particular [middle school] library, but I did go in there to get homework done and stuff like that." Isis said that in middle school, Miss Washington taught the students about how to cite their sources, which indicated a shift in how students interacted with their librarians between elementary school and middle school. As Jada highlighted, the library was no longer just about reading books and developing as a reader. It was about developing as a student, learning and growing. For some of the students, this might explain why they opted to use their public libraries instead of their middle school libraries. Both Trinity and Tahuti shared that their middle school libraries lacked the resources they needed, so they turned instead to their public libraries to support their learning needs. Furthermore, Tahuti's lack of engagement with his middle school librarian is also a significant shift from the relationship that he had developed with his elementary school librarian.

HIGH SCHOOL

All 15 students spoke about their experiences with their high school libraries or librarians. These experiences were quite varied, in terms of both library usage and interactions with librarians. As with the middle school libraries, the frequency of their high school library usage varied, as did the frequency and nature of their interactions with librarians. Several students reported frequent and regular visits to their high school libraries. Most students reported going to the library in class when they had research assignments, though only some students indicated that they learned how to use library resources, most of which focused on digital resources rather than print. Often the teacher would arrange for them to work on their assignments in the library, particularly for finding sources. Occasionally the librarian would provide them with instruction on finding sources and/or using library resources. Other students, like Jasmine, said that their study hall was held in the library, and Camaron said that teachers used the library space to hold study sessions. Only one student, Imani, reported regularly going to the high school library on her own. In addition to going to the library with her Advanced Placement (AP) and honors classes, she would go there while she waited for her parents to pick her up from school. She would do work for her courses, but she also used it as a place to work on her college essays. For most of these students, the library was a place to be productive. Jada described this well:

> I feel like working on a research paper in the library is helpful, because you're motivated to actually get everything done. Or else you're just doing research papers in the classroom, and maybe that's not the right environment. . . . I feel like libraries are very helpful because then you have the computer there, you also have the book. It's just better.

A few students reported little to no usage of their high school libraries. Just as was the case with his middle school library, Tahuti said that his high school library was underresourced. It sounded like he would occasionally be in his high school library, but it was not a particularly meaningful experience. He described it as "go there, sit, pass free time, and then leave." This was much different from his experience of libraries in elementary school. Isis, who was really engaged with her public and middle school libraries, also reported rarely using her high school library. She said the librarian would frequently close the library, even though students wanted to use it and needed her assistance. Isis reflected,

> She [the librarian] was hardly there. She would shut the library down when most students needed it the most. It was a real inconvenience. I think a lot of it had to with the fact that a lot of the computers were provided for us, but I don't feel like that helped, because a lot of times we would need the librarian's assistance.

She also mentioned that her high school, which was a technical high school, offered technology in the library but did not have much in terms of collections. Because of this, she would rely on the public library. Elijah, who attended a high school in a different country, reported that his school did not have a library. He relied on the internet to find sources for his schoolwork, noting that he learned how to do this effectively through trial and error.

Engagement with high school librarians also varied from student to student. Imani developed a positive relationship with her high school librarian through her daily use. In addition to supporting her schoolwork, Imani's librarian also helped her to write her college essays. She shared,

> She was very helpful. She was my go-to person for projects and reports and stuff. She kind of did more than just point me to different books . . . she helped me with editing my college essays. She was just very hands on.

Although Sekhmet's initial description of her high school librarian seemed either neutral or slightly negative, overall she had a positive experience with him. Initially she said, "He was quiet. He mostly kept to himself." She said he would "come out of his shell" for the "nerdier" students, including herself, but she did not view him as a good teacher. However, she shared experiences that suggested he cared about his students. "If there was a book that he didn't have in the library, he'd find a way to get it for us, [even] if that meant he had to buy it and then donate it to the high school." She also shared how he proactively engaged her in the library her freshman year:

> I was a shy freshman and I had no idea who to talk to about finding books and stuff. He found me just standing there looking at books going, "Do you need help?" And I said, "Yes, I'm looking for this." And then we just got talking about all the subjects that I needed to look for.

Most of the other students who interacted with their high school librarians reported that they were helpful when the students approached them with questions, but they did not go out of their way to engage with the students.

RESEARCH ASSIGNMENTS

We asked most students about their experiences with research assignments, though, in many cases, we did not have the opportunity to go into a lot of depth. Our rationale was that this might be a specific way in which they engaged with their school libraries, in terms of both resources (e.g., databases, books, etc.) and also the development of information literacy skills. Given that we, the authors, are academic librarians, we thought it might be interesting to know more about their precollegiate experiences with research assignments to understand more fully their experiences with libraries and research assignments in college.

The students' experiences with research assignments and expectations for those research assignments seemed to vary. Most students reported having to complete research assignments in middle school or high school or both. Elijah was an outlier because he did not go to high school in the United States. His last English class was in eighth grade, after which he mostly focused on mathematics and science. It does however sound like he did have assignments that required him to find and use information. A couple of students described intense high school research assignments. Jasmine shared a bit about her experience:

> We had this one research paper we had to do. I remember it was so much work. . . . They made it so serious. I remember my teacher [was] like, "Yeah, all my students, when they get to college, they tell me it really helped in college."

Several students mentioned that they had to do a lot of research papers in high school but did not necessarily convey that they believed that these were intense experiences. Others mentioned that they had research assignments, but they were not as serious as what Jasmine shared. Imani reflected, "I wrote papers and whatnot for classes, but they were very simple. The things I needed, I could easily Google." Camaron shared a similar experience, noting that most of his topics he could explore on Wikipedia. When Destiny reflected on her experience with research assignments in high school, she said, "Whereas [in] high school, everybody was lenient. Nobody really cared."[1]

When students spoke about their research assignments, in general, they seemed to be expected to use or preferred to use completely online sources. A couple of students shared explicit expectations related to online sources. Destiny said, "When we did research

assignments, we would have to look up books online. Like online books or journals but never physical books." We inferred this expectation or preference from other students, in that most of them just did not mention books when they spoke about the resources/sources they used. There were a couple of exceptions to this, however. Isis described a big research assignment in middle school, and they were required to use physical books and were not allowed to use online sources. Camaron also spoke about using books for a research assignment in ninth grade; however, it sounded like he relied more heavily on online sources as he got older.

Students shared what they learned about doing research assignments in high school. Many students mentioned learning how to cite their sources, and one student, Darius, mentioned learning how to use a particular citation tool, NoodleBib. Students also talked about learning how to search the internet and library databases, specifically mentioning Google, Google Scholar, EBSCO, JSTOR, and WorldCat. Two students mentioned that they used peer-reviewed or scholarly articles in high school. Jada said that she learned how to outline her papers, which helped her to develop a search strategy. Diamond specifically mentioned that she learned critical analysis skills. Only one student, Darius, mentioned that he learned about evaluating sources, but this was only after he was asked about that. Students learned these skills from their teachers, school librarians, and public librarians. About half of the students reported learning from school librarians through presentations or receiving help from their school librarians while working on their research assignments. Because his high school did not have a library, Elijah reported that he learned most of these skills on his own through "trial and error." His parents were university faculty, so he could go to them for help but noted that reaching out to them was a "last resort."

CONCLUSION

In our complementary special report, *Narratives of (Dis)Enfranchisement*, we described how residential segregation creates school segregation in contemporary K–12 public schools in the United States. Because of this, for this report, we analyzed the interview transcripts by the type of neighborhood we believed the students lived in based on descriptions of their hometowns and schools. Because school libraries were not the primary focus of the interview, we did not capture enough data for significant themes to emerge based on neighborhood. However, with one exception, the only students who mentioned that their libraries were underresourced were students who we believe came from more diverse neighborhoods. For example, Tahuti's middle and high school libraries did not play a significant role in his educational experience due to lack of resources, despite his elementary school library playing such a critical role in his learning. Likewise, Isis had a significant experience with her middle school library, but she expressed frustration about a lack of staffing and hours with her high school library. These experiences mirror the findings from Pribesh et al. (2011), including that school libraries with higher concentrations of poverty tend to have fewer hours available to students and inadequate resources. Destiny, on the other hand, who we believe lived in a majority White neighborhood, was not sure if she had a librarian in middle school. Students from both kinds of neighborhoods expressed the development of relationships with librarians throughout their elementary and secondary schooling experiences, and this did not seem entirely dependent on the race of the librarian. Instead, genuine care on the part of the librarian seemed to be important.

However, the overall lack of engagement with librarians, particularly in relation to research assignments in middle school and high school, is concerning and has perhaps resulted in missed opportunities for librarians to contribute to the students' academic growth and achievement. This was true even for students, such as Tahuti and Isis, who had developed relationships with staff at their public libraries or in their elementary school libraries. During the secondary education years, students are being prepared to transition to higher education, including in terms of their information literacy and research skills. Given that all of these students were matriculated at a selective research university, we can assume that they were academically inclined students throughout middle school and high school who enrolled in college preparatory courses, if not AP or dual-enrollment courses. Students reported that their teachers often taught them about finding and evaluating sources, although that instruction sometimes happened in library spaces. Only two students mentioned receiving explicit instruction in citing sources—Isis and Darius—both of whom learned about this topic from their librarians. As we discuss in the next chapter focusing on academic libraries, this likely has implications for students' awareness of the presence of academic libraries, their understanding of the expertise and support that librarians can provide during college, and the learning curve they had when finding sources for their collegiate research assignments. This lack of engagement could be due to a variety of factors, including school funding and availability of resources, teacher-librarian relationships, and librarians' individual explicit or implicit biases (e.g., see Brown's 2007 study). Issues related to race and engagement are explored further in chapter 6.

NOTE

1. It should be noted that these students were reflecting on their high school experiences after they had completed some research assignments in college, and they were often comparing these experiences to their collegiate experiences. Because of this, it is impossible to know if this is how they felt when they were in high school or if/how their perceptions changed over time with new experiences.

5

ACADEMIC LIBRARIES

All 15 of the students had experiences with libraries during college, though two of the students—Destiny and Trinity—reported using college and university libraries prior to becoming college students. In this chapter, we discuss the ways in which the students reported using libraries, including space and resources; their interactions with library staff; and their experiences with research assignments in college.

LIBRARY USE

All 15 of the students reported using The Ohio State University Libraries on a regular basis. Nine of the students shared the frequency of their usage with us. Although that frequency sometimes changed throughout the course of their collegiate lives, all but one of these students reported visiting a library location every weekday and occasionally on the weekends too. All 15 students reported using library locations to study or get their schoolwork done and noted that the libraries offer an atmosphere that is conducive to being productive. Camaron mentioned how the act of walking to the library signals that he is going there with the intent to do his work, and Elijah said that being in a library space reminds him that he is there to be productive. Jada shared how the design of the library makes her think about learning:

> I feel like the library is just . . . it's filled with books and it's a learning environment . . . that stuff just makes me think like, "Oh, learning, learning, learning," so I feel like that's just what makes me continue to come here, because I know I can be more productive.

A few students mentioned liking the camaraderie of being in a space with other students who are also trying to be productive and learn. Diamond said she prefers going to a library over other options, "especially since you see other people around you studying, too. It's really helpful seeing other people." The option for different kinds of spaces was also appealing, with some students mentioning that they like the comfortable seating options while others like to have the tables to spread out their work.

Eleven of the fifteen students explicitly mentioned they liked that the library offers them a quiet space to concentrate and be productive that other spaces could not offer to them. Many of these students reported having favorite library locations or spaces within a specific library that they knew would offer them this quiet space. Darius likes to go to one of the subject-specific libraries because "there's a desk where no one ever goes, so it's super quiet back there." Similarly, two students mentioned that the presence of carrels, which the students referred to as cubbies, signals that a particular floor or space is for quiet study. They also liked that the carrels helped to filter out distractions of other people moving around. Sekhmet listed various locations she likes to use, highlighting that "the cubbies are kind of my favorite." Imani indicated that if her favorite spot on the third floor of the main library was already taken, then she would not even look for another spot to study. The desire for quiet, focused study space was the primary reason students gave when asked why they use library spaces instead of spaces like coffee shops or the student union.

However, some students mentioned that it is nice having a variety of options among the various library locations or within a larger location. For example, Chloe shared,

> I usually stay on the lower floors because they're a little bit more loud, I mean, not quite loud, but a little bit more background noise than upstairs. . . . I hate going to the eleventh floor. It's so scary. I'm scared of coughing . . . like you don't want to disturb someone.

Some students noted that they really need quiet space for activities like reading, but it is nice to have some background noise when they are working on other kinds of schoolwork that does not require the same kind of deep focus. Camaron said,

> It just depends on what I'm doing. If I need to read something or take notes, I definitely need to be in a quiet space. But doing actual problems, like maybe if I was doing math or something else where I can listen to music and stuff, I could be in like a café setting.

Because the students used the library to concentrate on their work, library use was typically a solitary activity. However, a couple of students mentioned using group

study rooms or going to a library with a friend. Isis was the exception, noting that she really needed to go with other people to use the libraries to study. Elijah also implied that he was not opposed to his library time being a bit more social, stating, "I have a specific table that is mine, so it's very easy to find me."

Many students spoke about studying in the library as an alternative to studying in their rooms. These comparisons often came up organically, with the students initiating the comparison rather than the researchers asking specifically about this space, like we did with coffee shops or the student union. Camaron and Isis were exact opposites in their preferences. Whereas Isis said that "a lot of times I have to be dragged into the library to study" because she likes to lie in her bed with a snack, Camaron said that "I don't want to study or be stressed out in a place where I sleep just because you won't be able to sleep well." He also said that he does not like studying in his room, since there are a lot of other kinds of distractions there. Jada, on the other hand, tried to study in her bed when she first came to the university because her residence hall was not close to any of the library locations. However, she realized that strategy was not effective. She reflected, "Last semester, I used to try to study in my bedroom, and that never works. So this semester I've been trying to go to the library." She also noted that she's figured out the campus bus system, which has made it easier for her to get to a library location from her residence hall. However, she also mentioned that she has returned to studying in her room now that she lives off campus, though it was not clear if this is due to comfort, convenience, or both. Diamond stated how she finds it easier to focus in a library, especially since she lives at home. She explained,

> Since I commute, my parents wouldn't understand why I needed to drive twenty minutes on a Saturday evening and spend my whole evening at the library instead of studying at home. I would have to tell them, "I really can't focus at home." And if I do study at home, even if within those twenty minutes that I can focus, I'm going to stop studying . . . because my bed is upstairs.

She noted that the library's "atmosphere is very studious and it keeps you focused and awake." Elijah concurs with this sentiment, noting that he would often fall asleep if he tried to study in his room.

Most of the students reported using multiple library locations, and they shared different factors that determined which one they would choose. Not surprisingly, convenience was a factor, and students often used locations that were close to their residence halls or to their classrooms. Another important factor was the hours of the location. Some of the students preferred the smaller, subject-specific library locations because they were quieter, but these locations did not always have hours that aligned with the students' schedules. A couple of students mentioned how helpful it was to have a location that was available 24 hours a day during the week. Others based their decisions on the kind of work they needed to do and how important concentration was. The bigger, busier libraries had floors and spaces that were more conducive to collaboration, but sometimes they were too busy or crowded to permit that. One student mentioned that they liked to use the health sciences library for group study rooms, even though it was out of the way, because group study room reservations could be hard to come by at some of the other locations. Camaron talked about how his preferences in library locations changed over the years. During his first year, he went to the biggest library location on campus because that was the one he had visited during his campus tour. Over time, as he got to know the campus, he started to go to other locations that were quieter and where he was "guaranteed to find a study spot."

Students reported using the physical library spaces for reasons other than studying, though only a handful of students reported using the library for different activities. Students reported using the physical libraries to check out materials, including course materials that were placed on reserve. At least four students discussed how they use the libraries to access course materials, including some of their textbooks. Darius, in particular, noted how helpful this is in keeping costs down. Another student[1] shared, "I check out all of my textbooks for my classes from the library, so I don't buy them. I haven't bought a textbook yet this year." This student only found out about the ability to get course materials from the library since they began working at one of the locations as a student employee. They did not feel that this was well advertised. "They [the library] really don't advertise that, I don't think. Even professors, they don't advertise it, so now I do." Three students mentioned using the statewide catalog by name to request materials, including course materials. A few students also mentioned using the library to print or use a computer. Most of the students indicated that they had their own laptops or computers, but the library was helpful if there was something wrong with their own devices or if they did not feel like carrying around their devices. In addition, one student, Isis, noted that it was easier to use Excel on the computers in the library than on her Apple device. One student each mentioned using the Writing Center services in the library, coming to the library for a program or an event, and relaxing at the library between classes.

(DIS)ENGAGEMENT WITH LIBRARY STAFF AND LIBRARIANS

We asked the students about interactions that they have had with librarians and library staff while using libraries in college. Most of the students' interactions with library staff have been asking for help, checking out materials, within their classes, and as library student employees. Perhaps not surprisingly, the majority of their interactions were with frontline staff, including student employees. At least three students indicated that they do not intend to interact with other people, including library staff, when they visit a library. They are there to get their work done or to get what they need. Trinity shared, "Here we're interacting more with student assistants, and it's usually faster transactions, because I know if there's a line, you just get through it as fast as you can. . . . So it's like get your resource and go." A few of the students shared that they have friends who work in the library, so occasionally they will say a quick hello to them when they are there.

Several students reported that they have reached out for help when using the library, though as Elijah shared, these were not necessarily "meaningful" interactions. For the most part, students were asking for directional help—how to find a book on the shelves, how to print, and how to retrieve items that they had lost in the library. Isis was one of the students who has asked for help in the library, and she reported positive experiences. She shared, "The people at the front desk are really helpful. They're really welcoming. . . . I always get lost in here, honestly. I really don't know where I'm going in here." Imani, on the other hand, reached out for help with printing during her first year and found the experience to be "confusing," saying that "it didn't really help much." However, Imani does continue to ask questions when at the library, and she gave a few examples, saying "I ask a lot of questions about the online library resources. I'll ask in person at the library, like 'How do I do this on the website?' . . . 'How can I find this author if [the library has] it in stock?'" Tahuti was the only student who reported reaching out to a librarian for research help that went beyond basic directional or ready reference help. However, it is worth noting that one of Tahuti's family members had worked for several years in an academic library, so he might have some insider knowledge that other students likely do not have. Despite that insider knowledge, he shared that he was still nervous to reach out to a librarian for assistance. He recalled,

> When I first started out, I was nervous to talk to the librarians here . . . I guess the need of seeking help when I couldn't find it on my own. I feel like if I asked them, I was kind of . . . I don't want to say dumb, but kind of dumb. Like I should be doing that on my own. So I was kind of nervous to ask people.

Although directional and basic reference help is important, insofar as it helps students to get what they need to be successful, in general, students were not benefitting from the deeper expertise that many librarians and library staff have.

One reason for this lack of engagement was that the overwhelming majority of students were not aware that there are subject librarians who could help them. Nine of the students, including one library student employee, explicitly stated that they did not know about subject librarians, though most of them expressed an interest in learning more about these librarians. Jasmine stated, "I didn't know we had a librarian in college." Diamond knew that there were subject-specific libraries and assumed that those probably had librarians who could help with those subject areas, but she was not aware that there was more subject-specific expertise available to students. One library student employee shared, "I've never actually met the librarians here. . . . I have never seen a librarian come to the classroom." Malik also shared that a librarian had never come to one of his classes, and that he perceives college librarians to be more "standoffish" than the librarians in his public library. He said, "They let you do your thing. . . . Unless you personally ask for help, that's when you get it." Three of the students, all of whom were library student employees, did know about subject librarians. Despite this, only one out of the three had reached out to a subject librarian. One of the student employees shared, "I always suggest that [reaching out to a subject librarian] to people, but I never actually do it." Although this student was aware of subject librarians, they said they had never met the librarian at the location where they worked, seemingly unaware that many librarians work in that building. "I don't think they're ever there . . . they never interact with me. I don't think I've ever seen one."

Despite this, about half of the students reported that they had interacted with a librarian or library staff member through one of their classes or through cocurricular activities. Almost all of these interactions were within the first year or so of their collegiate experiences, with students mentioning presentations or workshops that we believe are associated with a required first-year course. Most of them did not share details about these interactions, though a couple did. Chloe had a positive experience when she needed to visit one of the library's special collections locations for an art class. She indicated that the librarian was welcoming and gave her the information that she needed to do her work. She said she would feel comfortable reaching out to that librarian in the future. Isis shared a positive experience as well, one during which she seemed to make a connection with the librarian who came to a bridge program in which she was both a participant and a peer mentor. She shared, "The one lady, I can't think of her name. Oh, my goodness. She's so awesome and she has so much energy." As Isis continued, it was clear that the librarian had been interested in getting to know her, and the librarian also shared some details about her own life, including some of the interesting fitness activities with which she was involved. Isis really appreciated how the librarian would recognize her and stop to talk to her when the librarian saw her around campus.

We asked students if they thought that librarians had expertise that could help them as college students and, if so, what kinds of expertise they thought librarians might have. Four students indicated that they believed librarians had expertise that could help them and were able to articulate what the librarians might be able to help with, even if they had not worked with a librarian in college. For the most part, these students shared that the librarians could help them find sources for their assignments, using both library resources and resources like Google Scholar. Most of them pointed out that the real issue was trying to figure out how to get to the right person to get help. Sekhmet shared that this was critical because "if the librarian doesn't know that subject matter well, she tends to make it worse, make it harder for the student to get what they need." Imani assumed that librarians had expertise, just based on the positive reputation of the university, but ultimately concluded, "I'm not exactly sure how much they know or how much they can help me." Other students really were not sure what the role of a librarian is and how they might help students. Jasmine shared, "I wouldn't know specifically what the role of a librarian would be." Diamond thought that subject librarians might be available to tutor students. One of the student employees thought that librarians select the bar codes for books, determine where books will go on the shelf, and do data entry. Although this student is not necessarily wrong—that is the work of many librarians—she could not articulate other kinds of expertise that could benefit her as a student. Jaylen said, "I never expected them to do a lot for me except check out books." Darius expressed a

similar sentiment, noting that when he checks out library materials, "I don't know if those are librarians or just college workers who hand me the books."

Finally, a couple of the students who worked in the libraries shared their experiences interacting with librarians and library staff, as well as with patrons. One student employee said their experience working in the library was overall positive but shared uncomfortable interactions that they have had. For example, noting that they would occasionally have to go to other departments to retrieve materials, and the student reflected,

> There's [another department] where I have to pull books sometimes, and I don't get them often, so I don't really know where to start looking. I don't know if [the full-time employee] is a librarian, but [they're] not altogether friendly. [They] kind of seem put out that you asked a question. I always feel bad at having to ask for help. I know that's probably just me and I don't want to assume anything about [them], but it hasn't all been positive to have to interact with [them]. [The full-time employee] kind of sighs, gets up, takes the paper and goes and finds it [themselves]. [They] really don't show you where to go looking and that sounds horrible. To be honest, most of the time if I have [something in that department] that I can't find, I'd rather mark it missing and have [my supervisor] go find it [rather] than trying to ask [them].

Another student employee also reported that their experience as a student employee had been quite positive. They said their supervisors were "nice" and "informative" and that it was a "good environment" and "chill." They liked that the students had a lot of autonomy and flexibility in terms of their schedules and said that they have become friends with many of the other student employees. They did mention that one of their supervisors was "mean," but they did not have to work with that person too often. They also mentioned that they occasionally faced microaggressions when working with library users, sharing that patrons frequently made comments about their hair. This student perceived these comments as "back-handed compliments. Like they probably think it's a compliment, but I'm just like, 'Why would you say that?'"

RESEARCH ASSIGNMENTS IN COLLEGE

We also asked most of the students about their experiences with research assignments in college to explore, from their perspectives, what their information needs are and how their collegiate experiences might be different from their high school experiences. For the most part, the students did think the experience of research assignments was different in college; these assignments were more intense and occasionally more stressful, and the expectations were higher. Camaron summarized the overall sentiment of the students in saying, "Longer papers and more sources"—and it was not always just the number of sources, but also the types of sources that they were expected to use in their research. About one-third of the students indicated that they needed to use scholarly and peer-reviewed articles in their research assignments in college. Two students spoke about how these kinds of sources were more complex than what they had been using previously. Jada recalled, "I noticed the ones that we'd been getting in college are a little lengthier and they're more complex, like vocab and everything." Camaron had a similar experience with the complexity of sources, noting that he was required to start using primary sources as a STEM student. The teaching assistant in his biology course took the time to explain to them the difference between primary sources, peer-reviewed sources, and review papers. This indicates an opportunity to support these students by helping them to develop the skills needed to find and use credible sources, in both their secondary and postsecondary educations.

Several students spoke about the intensity and higher expectations that they faced in college when it came to research assignments. Sekhmet said that in high school,

> They just wanted the overall general subject matter for it. You didn't need to go into detail. You didn't need to look that in depth into databases. It was just find the first thing that pops up and just write about

it or summarize it for us. That was really it.

Imani shared a similar sentiment: "In high school, I wrote papers and whatnot for classes, but the things that I needed I could easily Google. . . . You just have to use more resources and the work has to be more thorough [in college]." Camaron attributes some of this to "limitations to what we had access to in high school" in terms of databases and resources, especially when compared to a large research university. Destiny believes that her teachers were not as strict in high school when compared to her collegiate instructors. She reflected, "I guess it's more stressful in college because the stakes are [higher] and the teachers are more strict with their rubrics. And there's deadlines. Whereas [in] high school, everybody was lenient, nobody really cared." Tahuti noticed that students in college were expected to be more independent than those in high school:

> Probably just looking up books on our own. More independent. You have to look up research articles and use databases in college versus in high school. In high school, they kind of gave you what you needed. . . . In college, more, they told you what to do and you need to figure out how to do it and how to write the paper and research online. . . . They'll put it on a syllabus and we had to kind of figure it out.

Based on our experience, many instructors seem to assume that students have been well prepared to tackle research assignments in college based on their high school or early college academic experiences. However, our findings suggest that students' preparedness to do this work varies greatly, with some students having had significant instruction in library resources and research skills and other students receiving very little to no instruction about these topics, even when they were frequent library users.

Although none of these students indicated that they struggled intensely with research assignments in college, two students shared that their high school experiences had prepared them well and that the assignments they completed in college did not feel qualitatively different from those in high school. Jada took AP English in high school, for which she completed a lot of research papers. She said, "I took a Women Writers class last semester. We had to do a lot of research papers, and it [AP English] helped me a lot because I was like 'Oh, I know how to do this already.'" Diamond said the following about her experiences in high school: "[High school research assignments] helped me to form critical analysis skills . . . and it [doing research assignments] just helped me to learn how to navigate JSTOR and online catalogs, and how to go through different articles, like what keywords to type in." She said that she was able to transfer this experience to college, which helped with the transition.

Two students gave details about some of their experiences with research assignments in college, all of which had been positive. Notably, both of these students had the opportunity to explore topics that were meaningful to their identities. Isis took a lower-level environmental science course, in which she chose to explore the Detroit water crisis. She said that this project was "the coolest thing ever." Not only did Isis get to explore a topic that she found to be interesting and important, but she also got to share her findings with her classmates. "We all hung up our posters and pretty much explained our research. . . . We all met up at the [student] union and hung up our posters and presented our projects to each other." She concluded by saying, "I learned so much about the Detroit water crisis." Diamond described the assignment she had in her English course as "such a cool project." This was a community-based project, and students had to work in small groups to interview local Black visual artists. She said that the following semester the instructor shifted the focus to local Black business owners, which was something she was also really interested in.

For several students, instructors, not librarians, played a role in helping students to be successful, particularly in lower-level courses, by knowing how to access resources, including library resources. Three students—Chloe, Elijah, and Jasmine—said that their writing instructors introduced them to finding sources, including how to use library resources. Jasmine had a memorable experience, which she found

quite humorous: "And our professor, she had this whole rant about how we need to check out actual books from the library." The professor planned to take them to the library to show them how to find books and other resources, but it ended up getting canceled. Jasmine further shared, "She's like, 'Do you guys even use the library?' We're like, 'Yeah, to study.' She's like, 'Uh, you're missing out on so much.'" Jasmine's sociology professor told them that the library had a lot of sociology databases for them to use, but he did not give them details, such as names of databases or how to find them. Isis had a different experience in her environmental science course. There was a link to a research guide in the learning management system, and the instructor took the time to show them the link and then go over particular resources that were included on the guide.

PULLING IT ALL TOGETHER

In terms of library usage, the students in our study seemed to be aligned with previous research that explored Black and African American students' motivations for using libraries. The students in our study were all regular and frequent library users, and their primary motivation for coming to the library was to study and to be productive (Shoge, 2003; Whitmire, 2006). Like the students in the Duke University Libraries study exploring Black and African American students' library and campus experiences (Chapman et al., 2020), several students in our study also highlighted the importance of being able to check out their textbooks from the library rather than purchasing or renting them. Unlike the students in the Duke University Libraries study, however, the students in our study did not mention specific issues with library spaces that made them uncomfortable or that felt racialized. This may have been due to a difference in methods; we did not ask specifically about this, and we interviewed students individually rather than in focus groups. Another aspect of our students' experiences that is aligned with previous research (Shoge, 2003) is that they were not coming to the library to seek expert help. Except for interacting with employees at the circulation desks, the students in this study were largely disengaged with library staff. There are potentially several reasons for this. First, Ohio State is an incredibly large university, and, as several students mentioned, it can be difficult to figure out how to contact the right person. Another possibility is that the disengagement with librarians and library staff is cumulative, meaning that most of these students did not have meaningful experiences with librarians providing them with academic support prior to college, so they are unaware of the kinds of expertise and support that librarians could provide to them in college. Finally, as we discuss in the next chapter, race may also be an issue, in that students might see that the library staff is overwhelmingly White and might not feel comfortable putting themselves in the vulnerable position of asking for help. However, findings from Shachaf and Snyder (2007) and Hudson (2010) indicate that this student population might actually desire supportive interactions with the library if they are made aware of these services, even if the students are not actively seeking this kind of help.

In general, the students believed that research assignments in college were more intense and rigorous experiences than those in high school. However, none of the students expressed struggling intensely with these assignments as they transitioned from high school, as they have in other studies (Folk, 2018b). This might be due to their previous academic preparation, as well as the fact that they are ambitious, high-achieving students at a selective university. Transition experiences might be different at a less selective campus or institution, not because the students are less ambitious or driven, but because they might not have received the preparation needed to meet collegiate-level expectations for research assignments (Folk, 2018b, 2021). However, students identified some knowledge gaps in their research skills, gaps that instructors, not librarians, sometimes helped them to fill. In addition, many students indicated that the types of sources that they were expected to use in their assignments in college (i.e., peer-reviewed articles or scientific papers) were more complex than those in

high school. Although one student indicated that he had been explicitly taught about the differences between various sources, our findings suggest an opportunity for librarians to be involved in helping students understand various kinds of sources. We believe that the findings of our study lend some credence to librarians working with specific academic programs to support BIPOC students through the goals of introducing library resources and collegiate research skills as well as providing students with opportunities to interact and engage with a librarian (e.g., Clarke, 2012; Holmes & Lichtenstein, 1998; Love, 2009; Simmons-Welburn & Welburn, 2001). However, as we discuss in the next chapter, this recommendation must be approached with care given the overwhelmingly White composition of our library staffs and students' perceptions of White librarians (Katopol, 2012). Mortimore and Wall (2009), Pashia (2016), and Folk (2018a) provide some foundation for approaching this work, but more scholarship in this area is needed.

Although we did not cover these topics in depth in this chapter, our students did discuss issues related to a negative campus racial climate, including harassment from peers, failure of institutional support, and symbols that created a hostile environment. In the next chapter, which focuses specifically on the students' racialized experiences in libraries, we share some of the experiences that students had on campus and in university libraries and how those experiences affected them. Although the racialized experiences within university libraries that students shared were often not as overt as those occurring in other areas of campus, it was clear that the overall climate of the campus did not suddenly change when the students entered library spaces.

NOTE

1. To maintain the confidentiality of the library student employees who participated in the study, we have deliberately withheld the name of this student in this example. We will continue to do this throughout the rest of this chapter.

6

RACE AND LIBRARY EXPERIENCES

In our complementary special report, *Narratives of (Dis)Enfranchisement: Reckoning with the History of Libraries and the Black and African American Experience*, we argue that libraries in the United States and the institutions with which they are associated indeed have racialized histories, histories that have excluded and disenfranchised Black and African American communities until relatively recently. The legacy of this racialization, exclusion, and disenfranchisement has implications for how Black and African American users experience our libraries today. Based on our conversations with students who participated in our study, we argue that remnants of these racialized histories are still evident in their experiences with contemporary libraries. In the previous chapters, we discussed the students' overall experiences with particular types of libraries, such as public, school, and academic. Though we presented a few examples of racialized experiences, we did not go into much depth in those chapters. In this chapter, we share the racialized library experiences of the students, regardless of the library type, to demonstrate that libraries are, in fact, not neutral spaces and that Black and African American communities are experiencing libraries in ways that might be surprising to many White librarians and library staff. In fact, based on our students' experiences, we believe that White librarians and library staff are contributing to these racialized experiences either consciously or unconsciously. After sharing the experiences that students described in our interviews, we use critical race theory and theories related to Whiteness to unpack the ways in which White librarians and library staff are likely contributing to these racialized experiences.

Before we share the students' experiences, we would like to comment on data collection related to racialized experiences in this study. Willingness to discuss race and experiences of racism varied from student to student, and the race of the interviewer likely played an important role in determining the comfort level of the student regarding what they felt they could share. Seven of the interviews were conducted by Tracey, an African American woman, and four were conducted by Amanda, a White woman. Four interviews were conducted by both Tracey and Amanda. Where relevant, we will include information about the interviewers to indicate potential limitations of our data collection. If we were to do this study again, we would avoid using a White interviewer.

RACIALIZED EXPERIENCES IN LIBRARIES

Six of the fifteen students described racist incidents or racialized experiences in either public or academic libraries. None of the students reported experiencing these kinds of incidents in school libraries. Of these six students, four were interviewed by Tracey, one by Amanda, and one by both Tracey and Amanda. Nine of the fifteen students said that they had not experienced racism within libraries; three of these students were interviewed by Tracey, three by Amanda, and three by both Tracey and Amanda. Some of these students did share experiences with racism on campus, which is discussed in the next section.

Four of the students reported racialized or racist incidents in public libraries. Some of these experiences were not explicit or overt, such as Jaylen's perception that it took longer for material requests related to his Black or African American identity to be delivered than for other kinds of materials. However, other experiences were quite explicit. For Imani, this happened at quite a young age. Imani and her sister were participating in a summer reading program. They were waiting in line to collect their prizes, and Imani recognized how the White librarian who was distributing the prizes reacted differently to Imani and her sister compared to the White children who were in front of them. She shared,

> The librarian behind the desk was very abrupt and short with us. There were kids ahead of us in line, that she was like, "Oh, yeah. Good job for reading. Here's your [prize]." But when me and my sister got to the front of line, there was none of that, "Good job for reading the book." She just was like, "Uh, okay. You did what needs to be done. Here's your prize."

Imani further reflected on this experience:

> I loved reading. I always did that. I did the club every summer. I know [that] one summer in particular, I wasn't like a big fan of it, so I didn't go back to that [club]. . . . After that, my mom took us to different branches to get us away from that or just to show us like everyone's not the same.

Tahuti was also quite young, about 11 or 12 years old, when he had a racialized experience in a suburban library in a predominantly White neighborhood. He said it was his first year going to this library. Before that he had used public library branches that were in more urban and diverse neighborhoods. Tahuti reflected,

> I just asked them a question and they were kind of dismissive and rude to me. . . . There was a group of us, African American males and females, so I'm pretty sure they probably thought we were causing chaos and disruption. But we weren't. We were just asking a question. I think it was about printing . . . I had a question about printing. They'd be like, "Well, the directions are right there." They wouldn't come and help. They would just be like, "You need to read it and understand it yourself."

As with Imani, this had consequences for how comfortable Tahuti felt using that library. He shared, "So from there, if I didn't know the librarian, a White woman, I wouldn't approach them. I wouldn't go up and approach them and ask them questions. I would just stick to being quiet."

Sekhmet shared a racialized experience that she had in a public library as a college student. She attended one of the university's regional campuses for her first year of college, and this campus was located in a small, rural town. Sekhmet had been a regular public library user when she was growing up and noted that she had had positive experiences with White librarians in her hometown. She did add, however, that some of the branch libraries that were in predominantly White neighborhoods in her hometown were less welcoming of her, but they were not "outright racist." She said that her father described those branches as "hoity-toity." When she visited this new library in her college town, however, she experienced outright racism. Sekhmet said,

> I love libraries, so I always go exploring them. I was asking questions, and they told me to get out because this wasn't a place for a person like me. I was asking where books were. I was asking if they

had certain books. They didn't particularly like having a person of color in there.

Sekhmet felt that comment was true, not just of the
public library, but also of the campus and the town
as well.

Several students reported having racialized experiences in their university libraries, although, with a
couple of exceptions, these were not as overt as the
students' experiences in public libraries. At least three
students shared that they felt like people were sometimes staring at them or did not want to share a table
with them, even when the library was crowded. This
is behavior that they experienced throughout their
day-to-day lives in libraries and in other spaces.
Although this kind of experience is not unique to
libraries, it is important to highlight that Black and
African American students are experiencing this
behavior within library spaces. Darius shared, "I
guess at OSU it's like a joke amongst my friends and I.
It's like if we ever sit at a table, our table will be the
last one to get filled in the room." He said this was
also true of study rooms, that people would not ask to
use the room with him. Imani reported similar experiences, both when she studies alone in the library and
when she goes with her friends. She said, "When we
go at night, we'll sometimes get funny looks. I don't
know if people think like, 'Oh, it's a big group of Black
kids, they're going to be loud.'" She said that even
though they are not being disruptive, the assumption
is that they are going to cause trouble rather than
study, like the other students using the space. Several
of the students put a somewhat positive spin on this,
noting that they get to have plenty of space to spread
out or a quiet room to themselves. Destiny said, "I feel
like people would go to other parts of the library, but
that's fine, because I really like my space."

Two examples of more explicit racialized experiences in university libraries happened to library student employees while they were working at the
library.[1] As we mentioned in the previous chapter,
patrons commented about the hair of one of the student employees when she was working at one of the
circulation desks:

I mean, it's just mostly about my hair, because my
hair is super curly and big, so people make comments about that, and I would wear scarves and
people would make comments about my scarf . . .
like patrons coming up to the desk talking to me . . .
it's like back-handed compliments. Like they probably think it's a compliment, but I'm just like, "Why
would you say that?"

Another student shared negative experiences with
a White staff member when they would retrieve
materials from a specific area of one of the libraries. The
student said that they did not have to pull books from
this area on a regular basis so they would sometimes
need help. The student employee shared,

[They, the full-time library employee] kind of seem
put out that you asked a question. I always feel bad
at having to ask [them] for help. I know that's probably just me and I don't want to assume anything
about [them], but it hasn't all been positive to have
to interact with [them]. . . . [The full-time employee]
kind of sighs, gets up, takes the paper, and goes and
finds it [themselves]. . . . To be honest . . . I'd rather
mark it missing and have [my supervisor] go find it
[rather] than trying to ask [them].

Although this is a White staff member, the student
employee did try to rationalize that race might not
be the issue. "I don't know if it's just because I'm not
completely White. I don't know if it's because it's early
in the morning, and I've come asking questions. I can
just say it's not pleasant." Even though the student
employee indicates that these negative interactions
might not be based on race,[2] given the racial differences
between the student and the full-time staff member
and the student's previous experiences with race in
libraries, this adds another layer of frustration for a
student employee who is just trying to do their job.

RACIALIZED EXPERIENCES ON CAMPUS

Many students also reported experiencing various
kinds of racism on campus, and we believe it is
important to highlight these experiences because they
provide context for the experiences in library spaces

that students shared. At least five students discussed racist or racialized experiences in social situations, including in the on-campus residence halls where they lived. Chloe described an experience from her first year in college when she went to a neighbor's room to hang out and have a good time:

> They had like a little soiree in their room, and everybody was over there eating pizza and all that, and somebody had wine. One of the girls got drunk off the wine like really fast. Everybody's just chilling, kiki,[3] and having a good old time. And she's like, "You know, Chloe"—I was the only Black person in the room—"Did you know that my grandma had a black cat named N***er." I looked at her. I had never been so mad in my life. I was like, "Really?" And then her boyfriend, he like grabbed her. He was like, "Oh, you can't say that. You can't say that. What, what, you can't say that." She's like, "Oh, it wasn't like I was calling anybody that." There are others [other incidents], but that was the worst one.

Trinity also faced racist behavior in her residence hall, which resulted in her moving to a different residence hall. Trinity shared,

> Last semester, I moved out of my dorm because there were some racial issues on my floor. My floor mates were saying some things they shouldn't have been saying, and my RA was not responding to that and neither was the resident manager, so I just ended up moving. The response was like, "They're really nice guys. You should try to talk to them." And I was like, "Why would I want to do that?"

Trinity described the different avenues that she took to address this issue and reported that she either received no response from the people in charge or was encouraged to extend an olive branch and address the bad behavior herself. In the end, she was the one who was punished, having to uproot her life and move to a new residence hall. Other experiences with on-campus living situations that students shared include Malik's feeling like he was being watched when he moved around the small on-campus housing community that

he lived in, and Trinity's sighting of a Confederate flag hanging out of a window of her residence hall. The flag was eventually removed. Both Trinity and Imani spoke about the contemporary political climate with Donald Trump's presidency and how that seemed to embolden people's racist behavior.

The students in our study also described the ways in which race affected interactions with White peers or friends. Chloe shared a story about an experience with a White friend and how it ultimately affected their friendship:

> We went to the Columbus Museum of Art, and they had interactive questions. You write your Post-it note and put it up there. It's "What is something you care about?" and I put Black Lives Matter in all caps, and I put it up there. And she looked at what I was writing. She was like, "Oh my God, are you really going to write that? Is that what you're really going to put up there?" I stopped talking to her.

Jaylen shared how he felt fortunate to have interacted with a lot of White peers in high school because it helped him to understand how to interact with them. This was not something that was true for some of his Black friends in college. He said,

> I've been fortunate to a degree, just because I grew up in a basically Black school, up to high school. We moved, and I was basically in an Ohio State high school [in terms of racial composition]. I think that allowed me to kind of navigate how to interact with White people, way better than a lot of my friends. I've got friends that haven't been around White people much until college, and they still struggle. They're just like me, and they still struggle with conversations. Everything just goes the wrong way. So I think for me, I've been able to navigate that pretty well.

Sekhmet experienced a different kind of tension in her social life in college because she did not really feel like they fit in anywhere given her multiracial identity. She shared,

I've noticed that ethnicities tend to stay in their own little groups. They don't really branch out, and, with me, it's kind of hard to find an ethnicity to sink into because I'm multiracial. I hate to say this, but I'm not Black enough to be with the more African American side. I'm not White enough to be with the Caucasians. I tend to mostly get adopted by the Asians, but that's because I'm also part Japanese, so even though I am like them, I'm not fully accepted by them. So it's really me by myself. I'm used to that. I have maybe six really good friends, but I've never really found a place that I'm like, "Yes, I belong here."

Students also shared a couple of racialized experiences that they faced in their academic lives. Destiny said that if she is the first student to sit down in a classroom, "everybody would sit down across the room before they would sit next to me." Jaylen felt he had to prove himself and his competence as a teaching assistant (TA) to the White students whom he was supposed to help. He said,

I was the only Black TA. That was kind of analogous to my college experience in [STEM discipline] basically the whole time. A lot of classes, I'm the only Black kid. They are definitely reluctant to do anything with me, like when we have group stuff. Even with the students, I had to kind of prove that I was able to be a TA. In most cases, you have to do it [prove yourself when you are Black]. There were three of us, so a lot of them [the students] wouldn't ask me for help. Like, the Black ones would, because they liked that they had a TA of color. But, eventually, the White kids did too. Once I was able to prove to them.

THE ROLE OF RACE IN STUDENTS' LIBRARY EXPERIENCES

In this section, we share students' perceptions about the role(s) that race has played in their experiences with libraries, including interactions and experiences with BIPOC and White library staff.

The majority of the students had interacted primarily with White librarians and library staff, though several students regularly visited public library branches in diverse, urban settings and regularly saw or interacted with librarians or library staff of color. Several students indicated that they had never interacted with or met a BIPOC librarian. When asked to picture a librarian in their heads and describe that person to us, eleven of the fifteen students assigned a race to the librarian. Some students voluntarily shared this information, and others shared after being asked. Nine of the eleven students said the librarian that they pictured was White, and six of those students indicated that they pictured a White female. Two students, who regularly used libraries in diverse, urban neighborhoods, said they pictured a Black or African American librarian. Interestingly, one of these students, Trinity, spoke about the difference between the librarian she pictured and what most people might picture. She said,

I think in the mainstream, they're usually White. But, it's just that my library, the one that I grew up in, my community was predominantly Black, they had Black staff there. That wasn't necessarily the case for other libraries that you went to.

These students, for the most part, were acutely aware that librarianship is a predominantly White and female profession.

Whiteness in Students' Library Experiences

Although students did share negative experiences that they had with White library staff, overall their experiences with White librarians and library staff were neutral. In many cases, students reported having mixed experiences. Despite this, students did feel like they would have a different kind of connection with a Black or an African American staff member, which is discussed in more detail later in this chapter. Three female students, two of whom were interviewed by Amanda, reported overall positive interactions with White library staff but did not provide specific details about meaningful interactions they had. In general, they indicated that the White library staff they had encountered were friendly. Trinity, for example, shared that the majority of the public library staff who interacted with users were Black or staff of color, but the librarian was White. She spent most of her time "behind the scenes," but when she did come out, the librarian interacted with patrons, and Trinity perceived her as engaging. Jada noted how the White library staff with whom she worked as an intern would greet her and ask how she was doing, and Diamond shared how when she had needed help, White library staff responded "kindly."

Five of the fifteen students, four of whom were interviewed by Tracey and one by both Tracey and Amanda, shared more in-depth positive experiences with White librarians throughout their lives. Tahuti shared a positive experience with his elementary school librarian, a White female, who was invested in his learning to read. He reflected,

> She was very sweet. I know, me, growing up, I had a little problem with reading and writing. So her and my mom worked together improving my skills with that. So I spent some time with [her]. . . . She taught me how to read, and she selected books for me to read. She's very sweet and kind.

Both Sekhmet and Imani had positive experiences with their White high school librarians. Sekhmet described her White male high school librarian as "quiet," noting that he "mostly kept to himself." However, she said, "He was engaging to a select few students. The more nerdier ones, the ones who were more studious, he would be more inclined to come out of his shell for us." She spoke of a specific experience when she was in the library in her first year of high school:

> I was a shy freshman, and I had no idea who to talk to about finding books and stuff. He found me just standing there looking at books going, "Do you need help?" And I said, "Yes, I'm looking for this." And then we just got talking about all the subjects that I needed to look for.

Imani said that the White female librarian in her high school was her "go-to person for projects and reports." She added, "She kind of did more than just point me to different books . . . she helped me with editing my college essays. She was just very hands on."

Although meaningful or substantive interactions with librarians or library staff in college were minimal for the students, two female students reported positive interactions with White library staff at Ohio State. One of these students was interviewed by Tracey, and the other was interviewed by both Tracey and Amanda. Chloe was required to visit one of our special collections locations for her class, and while there she interacted with a White female staff member. She spoke about how the staff member gave her all the information she needed to access materials, including explaining why Chloe would need to call ahead. She said that this staff member was "nice." Isis was a bit more effusive about a White librarian with whom she had developed a relationship through several cocurricular programs with which she was involved. She described this librarian as "awesome," "interactive," "happy," "smiling," and having "so much energy." Isis described how this librarian cared about her, telling her, "You do so much. I'm so proud of you." To Isis, this was also indicative that this librarian would support her if she needed help, because they had "built that type of connection."

A few students highlighted the importance of geography, implicitly alluding to residential segregation, in determining the demographics of library staff and users. Both Camaron and Tahuti acknowledged that urban libraries tended to have more staff and users of color, whereas suburban libraries tended to be more White. Sekhmet spoke about how the demographics of library staff varied from neighborhood to neighborhood in her hometown, with the wealthier neighborhoods having predominantly White staff. These were the locations that her father referred to as "hoity-toity," because they felt less welcoming to them. Many students who visited predominantly White libraries felt that the staff were not proactive in greeting them, and they overall did not feel like they were being engaged. While these might not be explicitly or overtly racialized experiences, such accounts do suggest that certain libraries might be considered White spaces. Indeed, Tahuti went into detail about how he felt when he entered a library that he perceived to be White and his discomfort in approaching White library staff:

> When I go to the suburban library, I'm more tense. I'm not relaxed and feel like I can say things. I kind of go in, find what I need to do or do what I need to do, and kind of get out. Just the environment of just being a Black male and also in a White area. Just the stereotype of me making a disturbance. . . . When I walk in, they're staring at me, and it does feel kind of nervous when it's really quiet and you can tell somebody's starting at you. . . . People are observing you when they should be focused on themselves.

As illustrated in the previous quote from Tahuti, the intersections of gender and race might be salient in libraries that are perceived to be White, particularly for Black males. This is apparent in four of the six interviews with Black males. Three of these interviews were conducted by Tracey, and one interview was conducted by both Tracey and Amanda. Malik and Jaylen sensed that White librarians were not comfortable interacting with them. Malik described White librarians as being "standbackish" with him, and Jaylen believed that "they don't really have an interest in helping me." Although Camaron did not talk explicitly about this, he did indicate that he had not had meaningful interactions with library staff, but his sister had developed relationships with library staff. This could be due to a difference in personalities, but it could also be indicative of perceptions of how willing a White staff member would be to interact with a Black male. Tahuti's elaboration on this was the most direct:

> As an African American male, it is hard to approach a White woman. Just the way our society is. Because

libraries are predominantly more White-woman led. I just ask them a question, get what I need, and kind of go.

Two students' interviews demonstrate a distinct shift in how they perceived librarians or how welcome they felt in library spaces as they became older. This is important to highlight, as Black children are not afforded the same opportunity to be children through their teen years as White children often are (Alexander, 2020; Oluo, 2019; Tatum, 2017). Tahuti had a meaningful relationship with his White elementary school librarian, but as he became older, his relationship with White library staff turned negative. One factor in this shift is likely the racialized experience with a White public librarian discussed earlier in this chapter. However, this is also likely to due to how the White women he interacted with in his daily life reacted to him as he grew from being a child to a young Black man. He points to this when he says "just the way our society is." Sekhmet discussed a similar shift. When she was a child, she felt that librarians, both Black and White, were a nurturing presence, describing them as "motherly" and "welcoming." She reflected, "They really wanted to help and take care of the kids and teach them." But she immediately shifted to her collegiate experience as a comparison, stating, "Here, yes, it's been different because it feels like if you have a question, just suck it up and either try to figure it out yourself or throw yourself to wolves and not get help." Like Tahuti, Sekhmet also had racialized experiences in public and academic libraries, which likely contributed to these feelings. She also shared her vulnerability as a multiracial person and her difficulty finding a place where she feels like she belongs. Another contributing factor might be how society treats her differently as a young Black woman compared to when she was a small child.

Black Libraries and Librarians

One of the students, Jaylen, said that he thinks that Black librarians and library staff, in his experience, are "more personable" than the White librarians and library staff that he has encountered. This theme is apparent in many of the students' interviews. The students perceived that Black and African American library staff are more proactive in engaging them as library users. Tahuti spoke about how he is greeted by the Black library staff at a public library branch that serves a predominantly Black neighborhood. "They're like, 'Hey, how you doing? Can I help you with anything?'" Trinity said, "Since I was such a regular [at the public library], they [the Black library staff] knew the kind of things that I was interested in" and would proactively provide her with recommendations. This was also true for Isis, another regular at a diverse, urban public library branch. Isis formed a relationship with the staff. She said, "The librarians know me by first name. I can show up without my library card, and, you know, they'll still give me the book."

Several students reported having positive and meaningful experiences with Black librarians and library staff. Jaylen had developed positive relationships with two of his school librarians, one of whom was Black and the other of whom was multiracial. He shared,

> Even outside of the library stuff, I joined some creative clubs and things because [of] my [multiracial] librarian. . . . The Black librarian, I definitely had a lot of conversations with her, and she was just very down-to-earth and open to me.

He said that he still goes to see his school librarians when he is home for a visit. Sekhmet also had a close relationship with a Black public librarian, but the nature of the relationship is a bit different from Jaylen's. This librarian is her mother's best friend, and Sekhmet said that she helped to raise her. She described this librarian, saying "she's loving and kind but also strict if you kids get out of hand or if you get out of hand. She just handles her job with grace. She's just really cool." Isis shared meaningful experiences that she had with Black and African American librarians and library staff at both her middle school and her public library. Isis's description of her middle

school librarian, Miss Washington, was similar to Sekhmet's description of her mother's best friend. Isis said that Miss Washington was strict and had "zero tolerance for certain behaviors" but also described her as being "motherly." In addition to teaching students important academic skills like citing sources, Miss Washington also joked around with her students. Even though Miss Washington was strict, Isis described her in a fond and appreciative manner.

Just as some students perceived some libraries to be White spaces, other students perceived some libraries, particularly libraries serving diverse, urban neighborhoods, as Black spaces. Tahuti was explicit in making distinctions between Black libraries and White libraries, some of which was discussed in the previous section. He said,

> I do appreciate that the public libraries, they give us resources and access, because a lot of African Americans don't have that access. Printing and looking stuff up and paying bills. I can tell the difference when I'm at a Black library, because they're[4] busy doing their work . . . compared to a White one. I can tell a lot of people are using that digital resource.

He also highlighted the visibility of tutoring happening in the Black libraries that he has visited. Because of this activity and the way in which he is welcomed when he enters a Black library, Tahuti shared that he feels a lot more comfortable in Black libraries: "I would say the Black one, a feeling of comfort. And in the White one, probably intense. Just feeling intense at that one." This comfort also extends to his willingness to engage with staff and ask questions. He said,

> They're more engaging, more comfortable. I can talk to them and I can relay topics to them and understand. I can ask them questions more. I feel more comfortable seeking [them] out [and] asking them questions. . . . So, I'm more comfortable with the Black ones because I feel like they understand me more. So, like if I'm asking a certain question about, let's say, race, they can give me more knowledge

versus just the book facts. I can get a little bit more personal with them and we can agree and disagree on stuff versus a White [librarian/staff member].

Although Isis was not as direct in making a distinction between Black and White libraries, she described the ways in which the public library branch in her diverse, urban neighborhood is a point of pride for the community. Her neighborhood was predominantly Black and low income, and Isis described how the library served that particular community. She spoke with enthusiasm and pride about a mural depicting prominent African Americans on one outer wall of the library that she helped to create by virtue of her regular engagement with the library. Because this mural is both by and for the community, it marks the library as a community space. She reflected,

That mural was very significant to me because that library was like the center of my neighborhood, and I used to go there to stay out of trouble. I used to go there to read, look on the internet. The librarians knew me by first name. A lot of the activities that I did was based out of the library. They had reading programs where you earned like McDonald's gift cards if you read a certain amount of books. I was also a volunteer, so sometimes I'd help restock the shelves and stuff, help with CDs. . . . I feel it was an outlet to stay out of trouble. A lot of our friends were doing what they weren't supposed to be doing. We spent time in the library, whether it was computer, reading, you know, so it was kind of like the center of my neighborhood and kind of like an alternative to some of the things, some of the bad things that were going on in my neighborhood.

She also described the programming and services that the library offered for her community, including arts and crafts, movie nights, GED testing, and a day care center. Isis spoke about the commitment of the library staff to her community: "No matter what happened or who died in the neighborhood, or, you know, if something crazy happened, they always came back,

every single day. It showed me a whole lot about their investments into [the neighborhood]."

Many students had either not encountered or not had significant interactions with a Black librarian or library staff member. We asked these students if they thought their interactions with librarians or library staff would have been different if the librarians or library staff were Black. Almost all of these students believed that the interactions would have been different. A few students spoke about how it can be hard to approach someone who is not like you. Unlike Tahuti, who spoke specifically about how hard it is for him, as a Black male, to approach a White woman, these students spoke specifically about White librarians engaging them as Black library users. Malik spoke about how White librarians might not feel comfortable interacting with Black library users. Chloe elaborated on this: "I feel that sometimes maybe they don't know how to approach somebody who isn't like them. And maybe they don't want to offend, or maybe they just aren't totally comfortable either." Because of this, many students felt like Black librarians or library staff would understand them better and would be proactive in engaging these students, or, as Jaylen said, "more personable." Trinity discussed this:

Having a race component does change things in terms of knowing what resources would be most helpful for that study. Also, just having representation of somebody else [like me] on campus. I know the [social science department] is not diverse at all really. So just having another face on campus, somebody who is well-equipped to understand that racial background, and who has gone through the education system, who may have other resources. So it's just, you know, about life and about the resources available to combat some things that are happening.

Malik shared a similar sentiment: "They're [Black librarians] understanding of you trying to get your education and will help you to the best of their ability."

Because many of the students believed that Black librarians and library staff are better able to understand them, including their needs and their experiences, many students also indicated that they would be able to create a connection with the Black librarians and library staff, which would result in a relationship of care. Elijah shared how this was not just true of libraries, but in many facets of his life:

> As I got older, I do notice . . . that people of color tend to take a greater interest in [me]. . . . They'll be like someone who would more strongly identify with me, who would seem to take kind of a greater interest in what I was doing or how they could be of assistance to me.

Diamond connected this directly to libraries:

> I feel like with a Black librarian, we would automatically form some type of connection because we are both people of color and we are the minorities, so we're trying to help each other. And especially having a Black librarian who's above me, you know, I'm a child and they're a librarian, it's different because they want the best for me. Because all Black people kind of look out for each other, because we are the minority. . . . Instead of just helping me find a book, we would really develop some type of friendship, relationship, connection. Especially if I went to that library often and saw the same Black librarian, then I think they would be much more invested in my academics and learning experience, and try to actually suggest books, know that I would like it, because they actually care. They would actually keep up with my academics and probably ask questions about how I'm doing in school, how I'm doing at home, and things like that. Things outside of the norm, they would probably ask, just to look out for me.

Imani shared a similar sentiment, describing her interactions with Black librarians and library staff as "phenomenal." She shared,

> I feel like the Black staff at libraries like to see Black students are reading and learning and trying to gain and acquire knowledge, so they're always very encouraging, and just like, "Do you need help with anything?" or "Anything you're looking for?" [or] "So good to see you in here; please come back again."

To summarize this section, we share a quote from Trinity:

> I think that's something that's really important, when libraries reflect the communities that they're serving. . . . I think it's really important to have librarians of color, because it's like a person to look up to, who is a resource and who can just talk to you about life in general. You know, who understands your background.

CRITICAL RACE THEORY AND WHITENESS

In this section, we turn to two theoretical frameworks—critical race theory and Whiteness theories—to explore and unpack the experiences and perceptions the students shared with us. Both of these theoretical frameworks enable the exploration of race in library experiences and the ways in which BIPOC library users may experience discrimination, marginalization, or discomfort. However, they approach that exploration through different lenses. CRT acknowledges that racism is a regular occurrence for people of color and centers the voices and experiences of people of color. Theories related to Whiteness provide a framework for analyzing and identifying how White cultural values and White supremacy shape much of our daily lives, including institutions such as schools and libraries. Theories of Whiteness can help to identify how we might change our institutions to become more inclusive and equitable based on the experiences that are elevated and centered through CRT. An exploration of the racialized experiences is critical to fulfilling librarianship's professed interest in equity and social justice because "the presence and effects of systemic racism are often hidden in race-neutral approaches to service delivery that fail to account for the differential experience of racialized and marginalized groups" (Matthews, 2020, p. 2). In other words, to create equitable and just experiences, spaces, collections, programs, and services, we must critically examine the ways in which race affects contemporary library experiences.

Critical Race Theory

Library practitioners and scholars have used CRT throughout the past decade to explore various facets of libraries and librarianship, including library collections (Bowers et al., 2017), library leadership development programs (Hines, 2019), instruction and pedagogy (Leung & López-McKnight, 2020), professional standards and guidelines (Brook et al., 2015; Rapchak, 2019), LIS research (Stauffer, 2020) and discourse (Kumasi, 2013), information theory (Dunbar, 2008), and the LIS curriculum (Gibson et al., 2018). The application of CRT to LIS provides an opportunity to refute the myth that libraries are race-neutral spaces. Given that librarianship is an overwhelmingly White profession, race might not seem salient for a majority of librarians and library staff. However, for people who are racialized in American society (i.e., everyone who is not perceived or considered to be White), race is present as they navigate their daily lives, including their experiences within libraries. To adequately support and serve our BIPOC communities, we must explore the role of race in their lives and their library experiences.

CRT has its roots in critical legal studies in the latter half of the twentieth century and was shaped by prominent legal scholars, such as Kimberlé Crenshaw and Derrick Bell. At that time, critical legal studies examined the ways in which laws and the criminal justice system oppressed and marginalized people of color. As CRT developed, it became interdisciplinary in nature and began to be influenced by and applied to other fields of study and professions (Yosso, 2005). Although CRT focuses on the role of race in the oppression of people of color, it also takes into account other identity facets, such as gender, ability, and socioeconomic status. Although there is general agreement about the key elements or core concepts of CRT, different scholars have framed and articulated these

concepts in various ways. Matthews (2020) shares the five core concepts of CRT in education that were outlined by Ladson-Billings and Tate (1995):

- Race and racism are defining characteristics of society as opposed to isolated acts or events of discrimination.
- Ideologies of objectivity, meritocracy, neutrality, and colour-blindness often shield dominant groups from identifying their privilege in ways that sustain power.
- Analyses must be interdisciplinary and historical to disentangle dominant ideologies.
- It is a transformative social justice framework to eliminate all forms of oppression.
- It centres and is guided by the experiential knowledge of those whose lives are impacted by every day and systemic experiences of oppression and injustice. (as quoted in Matthews, 2020, p. 4)

Yosso (2005) highlights the same elements in her work about community cultural wealth, though, for her, CRT is not just interdisciplinary but transdisciplinary. Bowers et al. (2017) draw upon Dunbar (2008) to highlight five key elements of CRT—interest convergence, microaggressions, counternarratives, intersectionality, and social justice (Bowers et al., 2017, p. 162). We believe that the following elements of CRT are evident in the experiences and perceptions that our students shared: racism as an everyday reality, the experience of microaggressions, the development of counternarratives, and the importance of intersectionality.

Central to CRT is a recognition that racism is an everyday and lived reality for people of color in the United States. Yosso (2005) explains that "CRT starts from the premise that race and racism are central, endemic, permanent and a fundamental part of defining and explaining how US society functions" (p. 73). Racism can range from negative interactions with people who are explicitly or implicitly prejudiced against people of color to attempting to navigate obstacles and barriers presented by systemic racism. One of the many reasons why it is important to highlight this reality is that many White people take for granted the ways in which race shapes the everyday experiences of people of color, thus remaining completely invisible to them, since this is not something that White people experience firsthand.

The students in our study shared how race affects their daily lives as college students and as library users. Several of the students shared racialized experiences on campus, including symbols of hate being displayed in residence halls and the use of racial slurs. Furthermore, Trinity discussed an experience with systemic racism in that she followed the steps to report racism that she was experiencing in her on-campus living situation, but the process that was in place did nothing to address the issue or to hold other students accountable for their racist behavior. The burden was placed on Trinity, who ultimately needed to move to a different residence hall. Sekhmet's experience as a multiracial woman who struggles to figure out where she belongs and to form close friendships is also demonstrative of the salient role that race plays in navigating everyday life.

Many librarians imagine libraries as race-neutral spaces; however, the experiences our students shared indicate that the racism they face in the world does not disappear the moment they walk through a library's doors. They also had racialized experiences within libraries. Several students—Imani, Tahuti, Sekhmet, and a library student employee—shared hostile interactions with White library staff, which the students perceived to be based on racial differences. The root cause of the staff members' hostility—implicit or explicit bias—is completely immaterial, as the outcome or result for the students is the same either way. Both Imani and Sekhmet stopped using a particular library location, and Tahuti felt incredibly uncomfortable using a particular library location and engaged as little as he could while still being productive. The library student employee found ways to continue to be successful in their student job at the library without having to visit a particular space and interact with a specific White library staff member. These examples signal the continued disenfranchisement and disengagement of Black Americans and African Americans in library spaces, as each student perceived that they were being told that they did not belong

there. The space was not for them, the services were not for them, and the collections were not for them.

A related element of CRT is the regularity with which people of color experience racial microaggressions. Originally coined by Pierce (1970), the term microaggression refers to the "brief and commonplace daily verbal, behavioral or environmental indignities, whether intentional or unintentional, that communicate hostile, derogatory, or negative attitudes toward stigmatized or culturally marginalized groups."[5] Dunbar (2008) describes how microaggressions tend to be "subtle" or "non-verbal" (p. 44). Examples of microaggressions include backhanded compliments, such as a White person complimenting a person of color for being so articulate, or subtle behaviors, such as a White woman noticeably clutching her purse more tightly when walking past a Black male. Taken individually, microaggressions might seem more like an annoyance and less serious than more explicitly racist acts, such as the use of a racial slur or the presence of systemic racism. However, BIPOC tend to experience microaggressions with regularity, and the accumulation of these recurring and frequent experiences is what makes them so insidious. Oluo (2019) writes, "The cumulative effect of these constant reminders that you are 'less than' does real psychological damage. Regular exposure to microaggressions causes a person of color to feel isolated and invalidated" (p. 169). Furthermore, "They normalize racism. They make racist assumptions a part of everyday life" (Oluo, 2019, p. 172).

The students provided many examples of microaggressions that they have faced on campus and in different kinds of libraries. On campus, students shared that they sometimes feel like they are being watched, that other students do not want to sit next to them in the classroom or on the bus, and that some people will cross the street to avoid them. They reported experiencing similar microaggressions in library spaces, particularly in public and academic libraries. Students reported feeling watched by staff and their peers when using libraries, including when a small group of Black and African American students study together, as well as their peers not wanting to sit with them at tables or in small study rooms. Jaylen perceived that it took longer for his public library to fulfill requests for materials that were related to his identity, and that the interactions he had with librarians indicated they were not interested in helping him. One of the library student employees shared microaggressions that she experienced as a student employee staffing a circulation desk, receiving frequent comments about her hair. While these microaggressions did not seem to affect the frequency with which the students visited library spaces, it was understandably disturbing to some of them to feel like they were being watched and made them uncomfortable in those spaces. For some of the students, however, these microaggressions resulted in them not feeling comfortable asking for help in a library.

Another key element of CRT that is evident in our students' experiences is that of counternarratives or counterstories. Counternarratives often present a different perspective on the dominant narratives primarily constructed by Whites. On the one hand, this research study is a type of counternarrative, in that it seeks to share, elevate, and honor the stories and experiences of a student population whose voices are not typically consulted or elevated in the LIS literature. On the other hand, evidence suggests that some of the students are using counternarratives to highlight the positive aspects of their communities and their libraries. We see this most strongly in the experiences of Isis and Tahuti, who talk positively about their experiences with Black libraries.

Isis is aware of the perception that many people have about her low-income, diverse, urban community. Though she did not go into depth, she spoke about violence in the community and discussed how youth tend to get into trouble. However, she also painted the public library as a vibrant, supportive, community-centered institution, one of which she is quite proud. She talked about the supportive relationships she has developed with the library staff and the community-oriented programming and services that they provide. She spoke in depth about the mural depicting prominent Black and African American historical figures that is meant to be a source of uplift for

the community and about how the library was a source of refuge for many youth in the community. While dominant discourse about her neighborhood might focus on the negative aspects of the community, Isis painted a portrait of neighborhood pride in her public library. Tahuti, on the other hand, provided a contrast between what he categorizes as White libraries and Black libraries. He shared his awareness of how the White librarians with whom he has interacted perceive someone who looks like him, resulting in a cold, uncomfortable atmosphere when he is in White libraries. As a contrast, he discussed how the staff in Black libraries are welcoming and helpful, and he talked about all of the activity that he sees with users engaging with resources and staff.

Another example of counternarratives among the students is related to perceptions or descriptions of both real and hypothetical/imagined Black and African American librarians. Although none of the students reported being familiar with the racial demographics of the library profession, all but two of the students perceived librarians as being White. Trinity was intentional in breaking from the dominant narrative of librarians being White when she said,

> I think in the mainstream, they're usually White. But, it's just that my library, the one that I grew up in, my community was predominantly Black, they had Black staff there. That wasn't necessarily the case for other libraries that you went to.

She understood that librarians tend to be White, but she offered an experience that is different from the "mainstream." Students also spoke about their positive experiences with Black librarians and library staff, providing counternarratives to the negative, false, and harmful stereotypes held by many White people, such as Black people being angry, physically intimidating, or uninterested in academic pursuits. Many students characterized the Black librarians and library staff with whom they have interacted as engaging, personable, and welcoming. Students who had not had the opportunity to interact with Black librarians or library staff hypothesized that if they had, the experiences would have been positive, and the Black librarians or library staff would care about them as individuals and invest in their success.

Finally, the students' experiences in libraries highlight the importance of *intersectionality*, another key element of CRT that we believe is relevant to the findings of this study. A term coined by Crenshaw (1989), intersectionality acknowledges that race alone does not affect how one experiences the world. Rather, individuals have multiple salient facets of their identities, such as gender, sexuality, religious beliefs, or socioeconomic status, all of which intersect and shape how one experiences the world. For example, four of the six males who participated in the study described how they perceived that White librarians, in some cases female librarians, were not comfortable interacting with them. This again could be due to false and harmful stereotypes about Black males, particularly in this age of mass incarceration in which many White Americans equate criminality with Black masculinity (Alexander, 2020). This harmful stereotype is reinforced through media and popular culture. Another example is the library student employee who received many comments on her natural hair while working at a service point in the library. Black and African American women often experience microaggressions or receive negative feedback about their hair when they wear it naturally, as some White people perceive it to be unprofessional and others fetishize it as being exotic.

By sharing the experiences of the students and using CRT as a framework for analysis, our intention is to highlight that library spaces are not race neutral for our communities of color. Unfortunately, the societal stigma of race does not simply disappear when BIPOC users enter a library space. Students shared stories of explicit racism and microaggressions within library spaces that are similar to experiences in other aspects of their lives. The students were aware of stereotypes and biases, and many either explicitly or implicitly provided counternarratives about their experiences in libraries or with librarians and library staff. Finally, the ways in which Black and African American students experience libraries might vary based on other facets of their identities, such as gender.

Whiteness

Another theoretical frame that is increasingly being used in LIS scholarship is Whiteness. Different theories of Whiteness have been used to explore the nature of libraries and librarianship (Brook et al., 2015; Espinal, 2001; Galvan, 2015; Pawley, 2006; Schlesselman-Tarango, 2016; Warner, 2001), reference services (Hathcock & Sendaula, 2017), archival work (Ramirez, 2015), library spaces (Beilin, 2017), and research methodologies (Stauffer, 2020). Galvan (2015) provides helpful definitions of Whiteness and discusses how it manifests in our behaviors, often unbeknownst to White people. She writes, "Whiteness is 'ideology based on beliefs, values behaviors, habits and attitudes, which result in the unequal distribution of power and privilege.' . . . Beliefs, values behaviors, habits, and attitudes become gestures, enactments, and unconsciously repetitive acts which reinforce hegemony" (Defining Whiteness, para. 2). Often both the abstract and behavioral elements of Whiteness remain invisible to many White people because White people typically do not go through the same racial identity development that people of color do and therefore do not think of themselves in racialized terms (Tatum, 2017). In other words, they often do not reflect upon their own race and how it manifests through daily activities or systemically through social institutions, like schools and libraries. Also, through centuries of White-dominated discourse, Whiteness has become the unquestioned status quo in society in the United States.

Feagin (2020) provides a comprehensive overview and discussion of how Whiteness has become the dominant ideology in the United States through the concept of the White racial frame. Although the White racial frame predates the colonization of the territory that we now call the United States, Feagin highlights the centrality of the subordination and dehumanization of Native Americans, Black Americans, and African Americans through land theft and enslavement to the beginnings of the United States. Both of these cruel practices were central to the economic prosperity of the White colonizers, and it was therefore critical to perpetuate the superiority of Whites, particularly men, as a justification for the ways in which they were treating Native Americans and African Americans. Although enslavement ended in the late 1800s, other practices, including Jim Crow laws and redlining, were used to continue the subordination of Black and African American citizens. Even today, as we arguably are attempting to move toward a more inclusive and just society, the racial hierarchy that has White people at the top and Black and African American citizens at the bottom is maintained by individuals' beliefs and prejudices as well as institutions and systems that were designed to privilege White citizens. Feagin argues that many view the institutionalization of this racial hierarchy as the "routine organizational operation of society" (Feagin, 2020, p. 168), which is how systemic racism remains unchallenged and persists to the present day.

One framework to explore and analyze the manifestation of Whiteness in institutions, such as schools and libraries, is the concept of White institutional presence (WIP; Gusa, 2010), which was first introduced in the LIS literature by Brook et al. (2015). Gusa (2010) defines WIP as the "customary ideologies and practices rooted in the institution's design and the organization of its environment and activities" (p. 467). In other words, WIP allows for an examination of the taken-for-granted practices, systems, and values that largely go unexamined, because Whiteness often remains invisible to White people and is often treated as the status quo or the normal modus operandi. Gusa offers four characteristics of WIP:

- White ascendancy—This includes elements of superiority and entitlement based on "Whiteness's historical position of power and domination" (Gusa, 2010, p. 472).
- Monoculturalism—This asserts that cultural values, including the creation of knowledge, related to Whiteness are correct and objective. In other words, there is only one acceptable appropriate way of thinking or acting.

- White blindness (i.e., race invisibility)[6]—This makes discussions about race inappropriate and preserves White people's emotional comfort, as well as their White privilege.
- White estrangement—This is the "distancing of Whites physically and socially from people of color," thus making cross-racial interactions difficult, tense, and uncomfortable (Gusa, 2010, p. 478).

In our study, we see evidence of all four frames, and we provide examples in the discussion that follows. Many of the examples that we share do not fit neatly into a single frame, and elements of multiple frames are often evident in a single example.

The entitlement that accompanies White ascendancy includes "a sense of ownership White people may assume over a space" (Gusa, 2010, p. 472). This sense of entitlement is evident across the majority of the students' interviews, though it manifests in different ways. This is more overt and direct in the interactions with White librarians in public libraries that Imani, Sekhmet, and Tahuti described. In these cases, each student perceived that they were being told that they did not belong in this space. A subtler form of this is the fact that many students felt like they were being watched by White library staff or peers or perceived that White peers did not want to share tables or study rooms with them. These subtler acts of entitlement reinforce to the Black and African American students that they might be considered outsiders in library spaces. One aspect of White ascendency that was not significantly addressed in our study is the presence of security and/or police in libraries; however, Isis did mention that there was a Black security guard at her hometown public library and how important she believes it is for security guards to be welcoming of and friendly with library users. However, as Robinson (2019) points out, security presence in library spaces can reinforce for people of color that they are not welcome or that they are being watched, even though White library staff and users may believe that this presence is not problematic and ensures the safety of all.

In our students' experiences, examples of monoculturalism and race invisibility seem to overlap, and White ascendency also seems to be a potential contributor. In these examples, students felt like they had difficulty getting the materials or help that they needed. This could be rooted in monoculturalism, in that the students perceived that library staff valued White ways of knowing or that these students' needs were less important than those of other library users. For example, Jaylen perceived that materials he requested related to his Black/African American identity took longer to arrive than other materials he requested. However, it could also be based on race invisibility, in that White library staff were uncomfortable addressing race-related topics, especially with a Black or African American library user. Tahuti felt like he could not have a conversation with White librarians about topics that he might explore related to his racial identity. He said,

> I can get a little more personal with them [a Black librarian] and we can agree and disagree on stuff versus a White [librarian] . . . I wouldn't ask them [a White librarian], "Why do you recommend this book . . . and why is it important?"

He felt like it would not be appropriate for him to ask questions of the recommendations that the White librarian made for his research, but he said he would feel comfortable having these kinds of in-depth exchanges with a Black librarian. These perspectives and experiences indicate an urgent need for more BIPOC representation in the profession to ensure that we are adequately meeting the needs of our BIPOC users. Furthermore, many students reported having positive experiences or holding positive beliefs about Black and African American librarians, which further indicates that representation is a critical component of creating an inclusive library environment for this population.

There were multiple examples related to White estrangement in our study. Tahuti's categorization of White libraries and Black libraries is one example of this. A key element of Tahuti's categorization is the uncomfortable interactions that he has had with White librarians, particularly White female librarians. This was an experience that was echoed in several interviews, including Imani's experience receiving her summer reading prize and Jaylen's perception that White librarians do not have an interest in helping him. Several students also acknowledged how the racial composition of library employees seemed to vary based on the location of the library. Many students in the study who regularly visited libraries in predominantly White neighborhoods and communities reported that the librarians and library staff were not proactive in engaging them, such as telling them about library programming or providing readers' advisory, and some students attributed this to White librarians not feeling comfortable or knowing how to interact with users of a different race. Students who imagined what it would be like to interact with Black or African American librarians or library staff believed that they would be able to connect with them on a different level, on a meaningful level. Despite this, there were a few examples of cross-racial interactions and relationships between the students and library staff. In these situations, the White librarians and library staff showed a genuine interest in getting to know the students and supporting them. Because of this, the students seemed like they were able to trust those librarians and library staff enough to develop a relationship.

CONCLUSION

In this chapter we highlighted the racialized experiences that the students in our study described to us, both in libraries and in their daily lives as college students. Because librarianship is an overwhelmingly White profession, many librarians and library staff are likely unaware of the various ways that race affects the daily lives of our BIPOC library users. Other scholars have highlighted the problematic assumption that libraries are race-neutral spaces based on our professional mission and/or commitment to support and serve our communities, many of which have diverse demographics (Gibson et al., 2017; Honma, 2005). The experiences that our students shared indicate that libraries are not race-neutral spaces. The implicit and explicit biases of library employees do not simply disappear the moment they enter the library. It is unreasonable to expect that biases which exist in other facets of library employees' lives do not manifest when they are working or interacting with Black and African American community members. Likewise, Black and African American community members bring their experiences with White people with them into library spaces, and there is no reason to expect that they believe that their experiences with libraries are somehow going to be different from those in other places and spaces that they regularly visit, such as schools, doctors, or grocery stores.

We presented two frameworks to explore these experiences and provide some insight into factors that contribute to them. CRT and theories of Whiteness, such as WIP, are good complements, especially for a profession that is overwhelmingly White and has resisted, for the most part, explorations of Black and African American library users' experiences. CRT provides some insight into the experiences of people of color, experiences that White people typically do not have. It reminds us to center, elevate, believe, and honor the lived experiences and voices of people of color. When we do this and truly listen, we are gifted opportunities to improve our services, spaces, collections, and programming to support our communities. In this way, we can take steps to become more equitable and just organizations. Theories of Whiteness, including WIP, illuminate the ways in which Whiteness manifests and can be toxic. The manifestation of Whiteness is likely invisible to many White librarians and library staff because White cultural values are taken for granted, particularly those embedded in organizational culture, and are either tacitly or explicitly considered to be the status quo or the normal way of operating. However, this status quo can be injurious to our Black and African American community

members, as well as other communities of color, in that their identities can be marginalized by our behaviors, our spaces, and our services. In other words, unexamined Whiteness and its consequences maintains White supremacy and toxicity. Even if this maintenance is unintentional, the result for our communities of color is still harmful. WIP, in particular, provides four elements that can be used to analyze and interrogate our organizational culture, including our library operations and our spaces, to identify areas for change and improvement.

NOTES

1. As we have in previous chapters, we will not be using the student employees' pseudonyms to respect confidentiality. When possible, we will also exclude information about gender as well.

2. A potential reason why this student employee may have been hesitant to attribute this staff member's attitude to race could be that they were considering the potential collegial relationship between this staff member and the interviewer.

3. According to Wikipedia, "'Kiki' is a term which grew out of Black LGBTQ American social culture, and is loosely defined as a gathering of friends for the purpose of gossiping and chit-chat" (https://en.wikipedia.org/wiki/Kiki_(social_gathering), accessed April 8, 2022).

4. It is not clear if Tahuti is talking about library staff or users here. Either way, he is indicating that there is a qualitative difference between the activities happening in Black libraries and White libraries based on his experience with both.

5. Microaggression. (2021, March 26) In *Wikipedia.* https://en.wikipedia.org/wiki/Microaggression

6. We recognize the problematic nature of using the term blindness here, as it is ableist. We will refer to this characteristic as *race invisibility* throughout the rest of the book.

7

CONCLUSION

We conducted this study exploring Black and African American students' experiences with libraries because we realized there was a disturbing gap in the existing academic libraries literature: Black and African American students' voices were missing. Although several studies have examined Black and African American students' academic library usage, most of these used closed-ended surveys (Elteto et al., 2008; Shoge, 2003; Stewart et al., 2019; Whitmire, 1999, 2003, 2004). This survey research has provided an important foundation for understanding the ways in which Black and African American students use academic libraries, but the findings do not provide much insight into how Black and African American students *experience* libraries. Survey research does not provide the researcher with the opportunity to probe participants' experiences, perceptions, and feelings more deeply with follow-up questions, nor does it typically provide participants the opportunity to give detailed elaboration on their responses to questions. As we thought about developing a book that would go beyond the bounds of academic librarianship, we realized that Black and African American library users' voices and experiences were also conspicuously missing from both public and school libraries literature, with a few exceptions, which we discussed in our complementary special report, *Narratives of (Dis)Enfranchisement: Reckoning with the History of Libraries and the Black and African American Experience*.

The students in our study were regular library users from a young age through their collegiate years, and they had a diversity of experiences with libraries and library staff ranging from positive to neutral to negative. Almost all of the students identified as big readers from a young age, and their library usage was typically nurtured by their family members, including parents, grandparents, and siblings. Many of them participated in summer reading programs, book clubs, or reading competitions, but for most of them, that was the extent of their engagement with libraries. School library experiences varied among the participants based on the availability of librarians in their schools. Many had fond memories of their elementary school libraries and librarians, but librarians became more invisible for many of the students as they moved through middle school and high school. They reported going to the school library to work on research assignments, though frequently their teacher, not a librarian, instructed them on how to use library resources or how to find information more generally. These students were also regular users of their university libraries, primarily using them as a space to study. Though a few students had interacted with librarians and library staff in college, the students were largely unaware of how the people in the library could support them in their academic journey.

Our interviews with these students revealed that race has played a role in their library experiences, particularly in their experiences with public and academic libraries. Several students reported having positive and meaningful interactions with White librarians and library staff. In these cases, the White librarian or staff member demonstrated a sincere desire to get to know and support the student. However, that was not the case for other students who experienced overt racism and microaggressions from White librarians and library staff. Many of the students, particularly the men, felt that White librarians and library staff had been rude to or dismissive of them, perceiving that they had no interest in helping them. We did not interview these librarians and staff, so we cannot say with any certainty what their intentions were or if they were even aware of how their responses were being perceived. However, in the end, the librarians' intentions and awareness are not important; the outcome remains that many of these students had negative perceptions of White librarians and library staff based on these experiences. Several students who had not had interactions with Black or African American librarians or library staff believed that these interactions would be different from those with White librarians or library staff. These students imagined that Black and African American librarians would be more welcoming and take a genuine interest in multiple facets of their lives, and they, particularly the Black males in the study, indicated being more likely to engage with a Black or an African American librarian or staff member than with a White one.

At this point, some readers might be thinking that we are suggesting that White librarians and library staff are not able to adequately support our Black and African American library users. Although this interpretation is understandable, this is not what we believe. We have demonstrated in this report that our students have made some meaningful connections and relationships with White librarians and library staff. These relationships were predicated on the demonstration of genuine care, which is what many of the other students believed they would get from Black and African American librarians and library staff (and were not getting from their interactions with White librarians and library staff). To prepare White librarians and library staff to adequately serve Black and African American library users moving forward, we believe that White librarians need to undertake or continue a process of individual and collective learning about how racism and White privilege and supremacy manifest in society today and translate this into their work in libraries.

We also enthusiastically believe that our profession desperately needs to recruit and retain more BIPOC librarians. However, a deep discussion of this point is outside the scope of this report, and there is a wealth of literature on this topic despite the fact that we have not been able to achieve this goal (e.g., Alabi, 2018; Brook et al., 2015; Cunningham et al., 2019; Espinal et al., 2018; Galvan, 2015; Hathcock, 2015; Kendrick & Damasco, 2019). However, we believe that the point which we focus on here—intentional and continuous learning to be an antiracist—may also have a positive effect on the recruitment and retention of BIPOC librarians, as our goal is to help librarians contribute to inclusive, equitable, and antiracist organizational cultures. Furthermore, we believe the findings of this study indicate that the pipeline into the profession likely begins at a young age. Although they were regular and frequent library users throughout their lives, most of the students could not describe what librarians do and none had considered a career in librarianship. Furthermore, several students reported having bad experiences in libraries. Rather than starting recruitment efforts in college, we should consider all of our interactions with BIPOC library users at all points in their lives as opportunities to recruit them into the profession by cultivating caring, welcoming, supportive, and inclusive library environments, as well as by demonstrating the expertise that librarians add to their communities.

Matthews (2020) recently wrote, "Libraries are a racial space where the dominance of whiteness is sustained through unacknowledged norms, values, and structures that have operationalized white ways of being and knowing as invisible and normative in both our profession and our institutions" (p. 5). To move beyond the race evasiveness of the profession, we focus on the following call to action in the remainder of this book:

> Encouraging White librarians to commit to individual and collective learning about racial identity formation and Whiteness, including White privilege and supremacy, to consider how they can develop an antiracist approach to their professional work.

Again, librarians, library staff, and library organizations can take a number of actions to promote racial equity, including an equity-minded overhaul of recruitment, hiring, retention, and promotion practices; organizational learning (e.g., cultural competency workshops); and culturally inclusive and relevant programming. We do not want to understate the importance of these, but we believe that these topics have been the focus of many discussions in the profession.

One final note before we move to a deeper discussion of our call to action. The American Library Association (ALA) should consider implementing a Truth, Racial Healing, and Transformation (TRHT) framework (https://healourcommunities.org) and allow all librarians, library staff, and students to participate regardless of their membership status. ALA's divisions and round tables should be deeply involved in this work because that is where many librarians and library staff find their homes within ALA. Many divisions, round tables, sections, and interest groups have started smaller-scale initiatives related to equity, social justice, and antiracism; however, the profession would benefit from a more holistic approach to this, one that demonstrates an authentic desire to heal from our history to create a new future. ALA has had success with TRHT, giving support to libraries who offer TRHT Great Stories Clubs with youth in their communities (http://www.ala.org/tools/programming/great stories/TRHT). ALA should certainly continue to support this work but also consider how it could be applied to our profession in new ways.

KNOWING BETTER AND DOING BETTER: FROM ONE WHITE LIBRARIAN TO OTHER WHITE LIBRARY COLLEAGUES

In this section, I (Amanda) call upon my White library colleagues to commit to individual growth and reflection on the nature of racism, the pervasiveness of Whiteness, and what these mean for our profession and the communities with which we work. I am not speaking as an expert here; rather, I am speaking as a White librarian who is on her own journey to becoming an antiracist and sharing resources that have helped me. I'll start with a brief discussion of why we should care, talk about some of my own growth in this area, offer some basic strategies (though, again, I am not an expert on this!), provide some resources that I have found to be helpful, and share resources that Tracey believes will be helpful. Some White library colleagues hold racist and prejudiced beliefs and are uninterested in doing or unwilling to do the work to become antiracist. Although we can continue to try, there might not be much we can say or do to change their minds. However, I believe a good proportion of our White colleagues are unaware (as I once was), feel unempowered, or are overwhelmed. These colleagues are the primary audience for this section. If we can create awareness and help promote a sense of empowerment, we can make it more uncomfortable for our colleagues who hold racially discriminatory beliefs to enact those beliefs in the workplace while also attending to the needs of our BIPOC colleagues and patrons of color.

Before we dig in more deeply, I would like to begin with some quotes that I believe help to frame the purpose of this section:

- "In too many cases, educators do not question the assumptions they hold, and as a result, those who are charged with teaching, advising, and mentoring Black males too often inadvertently adopt attitudes and postures that are unsupportive and even hostile toward the boys they serve" (Noguera, 2008, p. xxi).
- "Our assumptions related to race are so deeply entrenched that it is virtually impossible for us

not to hold them unless we take conscious and deliberate action" (Noguera, 2008, p. 11).

- "White librarians should begin to develop an analysis of racism and racialization in the field and begin actively engaging in practices that seek to dismantle this legacy while avoiding the reproduction of problematic paradigms" (Gohr, 2017, p. 43).

- "White librarians need to develop an anti-racist analysis and apply it to librarianship, confront white privilege in its multiple manifestations, and work in alliance with librarians of color to dismantle institutional racism" (Melissa Kalpin Prescott in Prescott et al., 2017, p. 295).

- "Unless we engage in these and other conscious acts of reflection and reeducation, we easily repeat the process with our children. We teach what we were taught. The unexamined prejudices of the parents are passed on to the children. It is not our fault, but it is our responsibility to interrupt this cycle" (Tatum, 2017, p. 87).

In general, these quotes demonstrate the need for White allies who are willing to stand in the gap. According to Tatum (2017), "the role of the ally is not to 'help' those targeted by racism but to stand in solidarity with them, speaking up against systems of oppression, and to challenge other Whites to do the same" (p. 203). The distinction between helping and standing in solidarity is important. Our BIPOC users, communities, and colleagues do not need White saviors or heroes.[1] They need peers, friends, and advocates who care about them and are willing to follow or to lead depending on the situation. To be an effective ally is to stand in the gap for our BIPOC users, communities, and colleagues. Cooke (2020) discusses the multiple forms that standing in the gap can take, ranging from literally putting yourself in harm's way to protect fellow BIPOC protestors to being an active bystander when you witness a racist or discriminatory act, to being intentionally antiracist in your hiring process, and to honing and using your active listening skills. Many of us desire to be White allies who stand in the gap, but we have a lot of learning and self-reflection to undertake before we are able to do this effectively.

The rest of this section addresses some strategies that I have found helpful on my own journey.

First, I believe that many White library colleagues have a genuine desire to create inclusive and supportive library environments because they care about their communities and it is the right and moral thing to do. I do not want to get too philosophical here, but I do believe that most of our colleagues have good intentions in working with BIPOC users and colleagues. However, as illustrated in the previous quotations, most of us are unaware of the deep-seated and sometimes unconscious biases that we hold and how these manifest in our practice due to the prevalence of color- or race-evasive ideologies (see table 7.1 for specific details). We might be quick to make conscious or unconscious assumptions about colleagues or users based on the color of their skin that impact our interactions with them, and we rationalize that we are not making these assumptions based on a person's race but on other factors. These rationalizations allow us to feel comfortable.[2] However, our good intentions do not matter if they continue to reproduce racist practices because the results of our actions are still injurious to our BIPOC colleagues and users. They (rightfully) do not care about our intentions when our actions or behaviors cause them harm. Therefore, for White library colleagues who fall into this group, developing an antiracist mindset is in their best interest if they have an authentic goal to create welcoming and supportive library environments for all of their community members.

Each of us has a responsibility to develop an antiracist mindset, regardless of our position or role within our libraries, to achieve the goal of creating inclusive, welcoming, and supportive library environments for all of our users and colleagues. To do this, each of us must commit to individual learning, reflection, and growth, no matter how uncomfortable or painful. This growth is not something that will happen overnight or even in a matter of weeks or months. We have to be in this learning mode for the long haul, as it will take years or decades for us to undo the racialized beliefs and prejudices that we hold and to fight for equity for our users and colleagues. It is not enough to simply rely on diversity and cultural competency trainings

TABLE 7.1
The four frames of color-evasive racism as identified by Bonilla-Silva (2018)

COLOR-EVASIVE FRAME	DESCRIPTION
Abstract liberalism	"Using ideas associated with political liberalism (e.g., 'equal opportunity,' the idea that force should not be used to achieve social policy) and economic liberalism (e.g., choice, individualism) in an abstract manner to explain away racial matters" (Bonilla-Silva, 2018, p. 56). Common examples include affirmative action or busing to address segregation.
Naturalization	"Explain[ing] away racial phenomena by suggesting that they are natural occurrences" (Bonilla-Silva, 2018, p. 56). Common examples include monoracial friendships/relationships and residential segregation.
Cultural racism	Using "culturally based arguments such as 'Mexicans do not put much emphasis on education' or 'blacks have too many babies' to explain the standing of minorities in society" (Bonilla-Silva, 2018, p. 56). Common examples include equity gaps in educational attainment, income, or generational wealth.
Minimization	Believing that "discrimination is no longer a central factor affecting minorities' life chances" (Bonilla-Silva, 2018, p. 57). Common examples include affirmative action or social policies to address racial equity gaps.

provided by our organizations (though you should participate in those!). Instead, we need to develop an individual curriculum for our learning.

Early in my career, I did not think of myself as a racist, but now I am able to see quite clearly how my beliefs and mindset contributed to the reproduction of institutional racism and White supremacy in my workplace and beyond. I have always genuinely valued diversity and spent several years in college and graduate school studying other cultures and learning languages. However, I had not done the work to undo the color-evasive ideology that underpinned my beliefs about race. I have two examples that come to mind. The small liberal arts college where I held my first professional academic librarian position always held an annual convocation event. One year, Dr. Derrick Bell, one of the original thought leaders of CRT, was the speaker. I remember I was incredibly uncomfortable during his speech, left feeling angry, and was grumbling in my office about reverse racism and how White people are discriminated against too. In that short time frame, I exhibited all four of Bonilla-Silva's (2018) color-evasive frames and used a lot of the rhetorical moves he highlights as being common (see

table 7.1). A few years later, now in my second job, I was speaking with some colleagues informally at an event when a Black colleague brought up the issue of low pay within our organization. I was completely dismissive of her concerns because I felt that I was also underpaid and that this was not a racial issue, but something that affected all of us. Not long after that, I was promoted to a position that had more status, and it could have been an opportunity for me to speak some truth to power about the concerns of our BIPOC colleagues. I did not recognize that opportunity at the time.

Why am I sharing these experiences? Am I using this discussion as a therapeutic confessional? Maybe implicitly. My explicit goal in sharing these experiences is to say that it is never too late to begin doing this work. I was about six or seven years into my career when I truly started my journey of antiracist learning, reflection, and growth. I made mistakes, and I cannot change them. But I can know better and do better now and in the future, even though I will probably take some missteps as I learn and grow. So what changed in my life that I started on this journey? It doesn't have anything to do with race, actually. Just over 10 years ago, I met my partner and began a serious and committed cross–social class relationship. Until that point, I had genuinely believed that everyone had access to the same experiences and opportunities as I did because everyone I knew was mostly like me. After entering this relationship, I realized very quickly that this belief was completely false and the inability to get ahead had nothing to do with hard work and moral character. Our systems and institutions were not set up to allow everyone to get ahead. It is not true that everyone has equal opportunity, and meritocracy is a myth. At the same time, I had started a PhD in social and comparative analysis in education and was reading about racial inequities in K–12 and higher education. Everything just clicked for me, and I started to see the world in a very different way. If a White male like my partner could face systemic discrimination based on his socioeconomic background, such as teachers' assumptions about what his future would hold, then I fully believed that BIPOC people were also facing this kind of discrimination and worse. Having said that, I did not change as a person or a professional overnight, and my transformation continues to be in progress (and will be in progress for many, many years). I started to see the world differently, but I did not really know how to act on that.

Based on my own experience, I now share some topics and practices that I think are important for White colleagues to consider as they begin or continue on their own journey of becoming an antiracist. I encourage you to seek out advice, suggestions, and guidance from others, including experts, as we will all have different perspectives and experiences that might require different strategies.

1. *Implicit bias.* The concept of implicit bias really started to gain a lot of traction within the past decade or so, and it is possible that readers are already familiar with it. Understanding what implicit bias is and how it manifests is a great way to begin your antiracist journey, though implicit bias is about more than race. In general, implicit bias refers to unconscious attitudes, beliefs, or prejudices that cause you to think positively or negatively about people with particular traits and informs your actions or interactions. For example, this could explain how a White librarian could be unaware that they treat White children and Black children differently (though, again, lack of awareness is not a mitigating excuse). Resources are available to help you identify what your implicit biases are and then, using this awareness, to think about how to change your behavior. Project Implicit (2011) at Harvard University offers many Implicit Association Tests (IATs), including skin tone, weight, disability, religion, that are helpful in identifying what your implicit biases are. The Kirwan Institute for the Study of Race and Ethnicity (2018) at The Ohio State University has developed a series of modules that can help you work through and mitigate your implicit biases.

2. *Racial identity formation.* Racial identity formation was something that remained completely invisible to me until just a year or so ago. Now it seems so obvious that my BIPOC friends and colleagues explicitly undergo a process of racial identity formation, and that my own race has been completely invisible to me. Whiteness is normalized in our society; therefore, most White people do not have to undergo this same explicit process and often do not perceive that we, too, are racial beings. Tatum (2017) explains, "Whites tend to think of racial identity as something that other people have, not something that is salient for them" (p. 186). She offers an excellent overview of the process that many BIPOC youth experience (and ways to support them through this process), as well as of the racial identity process that many will undergo as they begin to develop an antiracist consciousness and the emotions that will be experienced.[3] I find that having a framework for understanding my journey is helpful to identify where I am in the process and what might help me to make progress moving forward. Part of this process for White people is "understand[ing] how the white racial frame is enacted in individuals' everyday lives" (Feagin, 2020, p. 143). For this reason, the

four frames of color-evasive racism as outlined by Bonilla-Silva (2018; see table 7.1) provide a good complement to exploring your own racial identity formation, as these might help you understand when and how your White racial lens manifests itself in your beliefs, values, and interactions with others.

3. *Emotions, discomfort, and the development of an antiracist conscience.* Discussions about race and racism evoke a lot of emotions for White people, at both the individual and the collective levels (Anderson, 2016; DiAngelo, 2018; Tatum, 2017). The many reasons for this mostly center on the feelings of the White person. If White people feel like they are being called out, they may believe they are being accused of being bad people or they are being attacked. I experienced this when I heard Dr. Bell speak several years ago. Even conversations about systemic racism (i.e., not about individual actions or behaviors) can evoke strong feelings because White people might feel guilt, shame, or anger when they are confronted with the fact that they have unearned privileges which have supported them throughout their lives and erroneously believe these privileges negate how hard they have worked. As you move along on your antiracist journey expect to feel intense emotions, including discomfort, shame, guilt, and anger (at systemic racism and possibly BIPOC). When this happens, stay the course because "if, despite the strong impulse to withdraw, the [White] individual remains engaged, he or she can turn the discomfort into action" (Tatum, 2017, p. 192). As you move through these emotions, you might have the urge to turn to a BIPOC friend, family member, or colleague for guidance or a confessional. This is not appropriate, and it is not their responsibility to educate you, console you, or validate you. If you need support, look for other White individuals in your family, your organization, or your community who are committed to doing this work (book clubs might be a place to start), or, if you have the means to do so, work with a counselor or therapist.

4. *Reflection.* Feagin (2020) highlighted the importance of understanding how racism and Whiteness manifest in our daily lives. To develop this kind of awareness, reflection is essential. One aspect of this is self-reflection, during which we take the time to analyze our own beliefs, assumptions, and behaviors when they arise throughout our daily interactions. In terms of the workplace, you might reflect on how you reacted when you saw a large group of Black and African American teens enter the library. Did you make assumptions about how they would behave or why they were in the space? What about when confronted by a person experiencing homelessness who needed help using the computer? Did you provide the same level of service to them as you would to other patrons or were you quick to dismiss them? We might also find ourselves making hiring and employment decisions. What kinds of assumptions did you make about candidates based on the personal information you had about them? What did you do to treat the candidates equitably? Maybe you accidentally misgendered a colleague and were gently corrected, but you felt a lot of anger and responded poorly. Why did that gentle correction elicit such a strong emotional response? Was the emotion that you felt actually anger, or were you feeling other emotions? How might you reframe your response to a gentle correction in the future? As you continue on your journey, you will likely become a lot more aware of how biases manifest in everyday activities and begin to consider your role in them. For example, I once witnessed four White women walk right in front of a Black woman (cutting her off, essentially) in a grocery store within a matter of a minute or so. Based on the way the store was set up, the Black woman, in my opinion, had the right of way. Why did these women feel so entitled in that space that they would walk right in front of another shopper? How often have I done this? How might these feelings of entitlement

meaningfully manifest in other aspects of my life? How frustrating must it be for that Black woman to experience this on a regular basis when she is just trying to live her life like the rest of us? Many people like to journal as a form of reflection, but that is not the only method of reflection. The purpose of reflection is to be intentional about carving out space for us to do the mental work that enables us to see how our biases, assumptions, and values might manifest throughout the course of our day and determine whether or not our actions or thoughts are aligned with our goal of being antiracist allies. Kendi's (2020) *Be Antiracist* workbook will likely be a useful tool to many who are interested in doing this kind of reflection.

5. *Being an ally.* As you develop an awareness of how biases and racism manifest in our daily lives, including our professional lives, it is time to take action and stand in the gap. As Cooke (2020) reminds us, being an ally and standing in the gap will take multiple forms and will change from situation to situation. An important first step is actively listening to your BIPOC users, communities, and colleagues about their needs and their experiences and advocating for them. You can also practice speaking up when you observe something that you think might be inequitable. This could be pointing out that an organization is requiring only BIPOC colleagues to do DEIA (diversity, equity, inclusion, accessibility) work, rather than expecting a broad range of colleagues to be involved. Or maybe a hiring committee is making implicit assumptions about a candidate's potential based on their name, assumptions that were not made of similar candidates who have more White-sounding names, and you ask why this candidate is not as desirable as the others. Sometimes standing in the gap in our workplaces is a bit more intense, though speaking up in other situations can certainly be daunting. More intense situations might be intervening when one patron uses a racial slur with another patron or being present and visible (and perhaps asking questions) when a security officer is handling a situation with a BIPOC library user. Becoming an ally also means that you will not always get it right. When this happens, take the time to work through your emotions (not with BIPOC), think about why things did not go right, and what you might do differently in the future.

6. *Realizing the work is never done.* Throughout this section, I have likened this work to going on a journey. Some might find that problematic because a journey implies that there is a destination, a place where you are finally at rest. To a certain extent, there is a destination: being an effective White ally. However, an effective White ally realizes that the work of learning and reflecting and doing better is never over—this is a lifelong commitment.

To conclude this section, I'd like to share resources that I have found helpful or that are on my list for continued learning as well as resources that Tracey believes will be helpful. Many of these have been cited or identified as recommended readings throughout the book. Most of these resources are books because that is how I prefer to learn. Some are specific to libraries, but most are about race and racism in the United States more generally. I realize that some of you might find podcasts, videos, blogs, or short articles (of which there are many!) to be more appealing and helpful. With this in mind, I also include some links to general resources lists.

Resources from Amanda
Helpful Books I Have Read

Alexander, M. (2020). *The new Jim Crow: Mass incarceration in the age of colorblindness.* The New Press.

Bonilla-Silva, E. (2018). *Racism without racists: Colorblind racism and the persistence of racial inequality in America* (5th ed.). Rowman & Littlefield.

Burke, M. (2019). *Colorblind racism.* Polity.

Clotfelter, C. (2004). *After Brown: The rise and retreat of school desegregation.* Princeton University Press.

Feagin, J. R. (2020). *The White racial frame: Centuries of framing and counter-framing* (3rd ed.). Routledge.

Grant, G. (2011). *Hope and despair in the American city: Why there are no bad schools in Raleigh.* Harvard University Press.

Holloway, K. F. C. (2006). *BookMarks: Reading in black and white.* Rutgers University Press.

Ioanide, P. (2015). *The emotional politics of racism: How feelings trump facts in an era of colorblindness.* Stanford University Press.

Kendi, I. X. (2019). *How to be an antiracist.* One World.

Knott, C. (2015). *Not free, not for all: Public libraries in the age of Jim Crow.* University of Massachusetts Press.

McGhee, H. (2021). *The sum of us: What racism costs everyone and how we can prosper together.* One World.

Noble, S. U. (2018). *Algorithms of oppression: How search engines reinforce racism.* NYU Press.

Noguera, P. A. (2008). *The trouble with black boys . . . and other reflections on race, equity, and the future of public education.* Jossey-Bass.

Oluo, I. (2019). *So you want to talk about race.* Seal Press.

Pollock, M. (Ed.). (2008). *Everyday antiracism: Getting real about race in school.* The New Press.

Selby, M. (2019). *Freedom libraries: The untold story of libraries for African Americans in the South.* Rowman & Littlefield.

Tatum, B. D. (2017). *Why are all the black kids sitting together in the cafeteria? And other conversations about race.* Basic Books.

Wiegand, W. A., & Wiegand, S. A. (2018). *The desegregation of public libraries in the Jim Crow South: Civil rights and local activism.* Louisiana State University Press.

Wilder, C. S. (2013). *Ebony and ivy: Race, slavery, and the troubled history of America's universities.* Bloomsbury.

Books on My Reading List

Anderson, C. (2016). *White rage: The unspoken truth of our racial divide.* Bloomsbury.

Benjamin, R. (2019). *Race after technology: Abolitionist tools for the new Jim Code.* Polity.

Coates, T. (2015). *Between the world and me.* Spiegel & Grau.

DiAngelo, R. (2018). *White fragility: Why it's so hard for white people to talk about racism.* Beacon Press.

Kendall, M. (2020). *Hood feminism: Notes from the women that a movement forgot.* Viking.

Kendi, I. X. (2016). *Stamped from the beginning: The definitive history of racist ideas in America.* National Books.

Rothstein, R. *The color of law: A forgotten history of how our government segregated America.* Liveright.

Saad, L. F. (2020). *Me and white supremacy: Combat racism, change the world, and become a good ancestor.* Sourcebooks.

Taylor, C. (2020). *Overground railroad: The Green Book and the roots of black travel in America.* Abrams Press.

Podcasts

Grimmett, J. (Host). (2019). *Learning, lifting, leading: Social equity for and by Black and Brown girls and women* [Audio podcast]. Kernodle Center for Service Learning and Community Engagement, Elon University. https://podcasts.apple.com/us/podcast/learning-lifting-leading/id1455222467

Resources Lists

@tttkay [Twitter profile]. (n.d.). *Black excellence in LIS syllabus.* https://docs.google.com/spreadsheets/d/1vV0j2RrAszGulihZPstj_8Rc2PCURYSpYqYQxFc6Yeg/edit#gid=674562782

Cooke, N. A. (n.d.). *Anti-racism resources for all ages.* https://padlet.com/nicolethelibrarian/nbasekqoazt336co

Cooke, N. A., & Hill, R. F. (2017). Considering cultural competence: An annotated reading list. *Knowledge Quest*, 45(3), 54–61.

JSTOR & Schomburg Center for Research in Black Culture. (n.d.). *JSTOR and Schomburg Center Open Library*. https://docs.google.com/spreadsheets/d/1kjor_SY_5A2wd95xuhLJ1SWCgyaoq5eSB7czJ7E7UVg/edit#gid=0

Rosario, I. (2020, June 6). This list of books, films and podcasts about racism is a start, not a panacea. *Code Switch*. https://www.npr.org/sections/codeswitch/2020/06/06/871023438/this-list-of-books-films-and-podcasts-about-racism-is-a-start-not-a-panacea

Strand, K. J. (2019). *Disrupting Whiteness in libraries and librarianship: A reading list.* The Office of the Gender and Women's Studies Librarian, University of Wisconsin–Madison Libraries. https:/www.library.wisc.edu/gwslibrarian/bibliographies/disrupting-whiteness-in-libraries/

TED. (n.d.). *Talks to help you understand racism in America* [Playlist]. https://www.ted.com/playlists/250/talks_to_help_you_understand_r

Resources from Tracey

Many of the resources that Tracey would like to share provide an alternative to the White-dominated, Eurocentric view of history that many of us learned in school, that many still learn in school, and that is represented in many of our collections. As we addressed in *Narratives of (Dis)Enfranchisement*, many American children learn that African or African American history begins with enslavement. This simply is not true, and it is particularly injurious to Black and African American children's self-esteem and their place in the world. It also builds a false narrative about Black and African Americans to other cultures, particularly the majority White society that has viewed and, in some cases, still views BIPOC individuals and communities as inferior or as a noncontributory people, thus causing current issues in today's society around race relations, including mass incarceration and violence against BIPOC.

Akua, C. (2015). *Honoring our ancestral obligations: 7 steps to Black student success*. Imani Enterprises.

Browder, A. T. (1992). *Nile Valley contributions to civilization: Exploding the myths*. Institute of Karmic Guidance.

Folk, A. L., & Overbey, T. (2019, April 10–13). *Narratives of (dis)engagement: Exploring Black/African-American undergraduate students' experiences with libraries*. ACRL 2019—Recasting the narrative, Cleveland, OH, United States. https://www.ala.org/acrl/sites/ala.org.acrl/files/content/conferences/confsandpreconfs/2019/NarrativesofDisEngagement.pdf

James, G. J. M. (2017). *Stolen legacy: Greek philosophy is stolen Egyptian philosophy*. Allegro Editions.

Rashidi, R. (2012). *African star over Asia: The Black presence in the East*. Books of Africa.

Walker, R. (2011). *When we ruled: The ancient and mediaeval history of Black civilisations*. Black Classic Press.

Walker, R. (2013). *Blacks and science volume one: Ancient Egyptian contributions to science and technology and the mysterious sciences of the Great Pyramid*. CreateSpace Independent Publishing Platform.

Walker, R. (2013). *Blacks and science volume two: West and East African contributions to science and technology and intellectual life and legacy of Timbuktu*. CreateSpace Independent Publishing Platform.

Walker, R. (2013). *Blacks and science volume three: African American contributions to science and technology*. CreateSpace Independent Publishing Platform.

Williams, C. (1992). *Destruction of Black civilization: Great issues of a race from 4500 B.C. to 2000 A.D.* Third World Press.

Zulu, I. M. (1993). The ancient Kemetic roots of library and information science. In S. F. Biddle et al. (Eds.), *Culture keepers: Enlightening and empowering our communities—Proceedings of the first national conference of African American librarians, September 4–6, 1992, Columbus, Ohio* (pp. 246–266). The Black Caucus of the American Library Association. https://files.eric.ed.gov/fulltext/ED382204.pdf

NOTES

1. Saad (2020) defines White saviorism as "the belief that people with white privilege, who see themselves as superior in capability and intelligence, have an obligation to 'save' BIPOC from their supposed inferiority and helplessness" (p. 149).

2. In fact, many readers were likely dismissive of the content in the previous chapters or in *Narratives of [Dis]Enfranchisement*, our companion special report, and are developing alternative, nonracial explanations for content related to equity gaps in education, the prevalence of residential segregation, or the discrimination that our students reported experiencing in libraries. Bonilla-Silva's (2018) color-evasive frames speak directly to this!

3. Many colleagues, including myself, have found the Summary of Stages of Racial Identity Development handout, by Cynthia Silva Parker and Jen Wilsea from the Interaction Institute for Social Change, to be helpful. It is currently available at https://overcomingracism.org/wp-content/uploads/2021/05/stages-of-racial-identity-development-oct2019.pdf.

REFERENCES

Agosto, D. E., & Hughes-Hassell, S. (2005). People, places, and questions: An investigation of the everyday life information-seeking behaviors of urban young adults. *Library and Information Science Research*, 27, 141–163.

Alabi, J. (2018). From hostile to inclusive: Strategies for improving the racial climate of academic libraries. *Library Trends*, 67(1), 131–146.

Alexander, M. (2020). *The new Jim Crow: Mass incarceration in the age of colorblindness.* The New Press.

ALISE Association of Library and Information Science Education. (2020). *2020 Statistical report: Trends and key indicators in library and information science.* https://www.alise.org/statistical -report

Anderson, C. (2016). *White rage: The unspoken truth of our racial divide.* Bloomsbury.

Annamma, S. A, Jackson, D. D., & Morrison, D. (2017). Conceptualizing color-evasiveness: Using dis/ability critical race theory to expand a color-blind racial ideology in education and society. *Race Ethnicity and Education*, 20(2), 147–162.

Beasley, M. M. (2017). Performing refuge/restoration: The role of libraries in the African American Community—Ferguson, Baltimore and Dorchester. *Performance Research*, 22(1), 75–81.

Beilin, I. (2017). The academic research library's White past and present. In G. Schlesselman-Tarango (Ed.), *Topographies of Whiteness: Mapping Whiteness in library and information science* (pp. 79-98). Library Juice Press.

Bonilla-Silva, E. (2018). *Racism without racists: Color-blind racism and the persistence of racial inequality in America* (5th ed.). Rowman & Littlefield.

Bourg, C. (2014, March 3). The unbearable whiteness of librarianship. *Feral Librarian.* https:// chrisbourg.wordpress.com/2014/03/03/ the-unbearable-whiteness-of-librarianship/

Bowers, J., Crowe, K., & Keeran, P. (2017). "If you want the history of a White man, you go to the library": Critiquing our legacy, addressing our collections gaps. *Collection Management*, 42(3–4), 159–179.

Brook, F., Ellenwood, D., & Lazzaro, A. E. (2015). In pursuit of antiracist social justice: Denaturalizing whiteness in the academic library. *Library Trends*, 64(2), 246–284.

Brown, T. M. (2007). Culture, gender and subjectivities: Computer and internet restrictions in a high school library. *Journal of Access Services*, 4(3/4), 1–26.

Burke, M. (2019). *Colorblind racism.* Polity.

Chapman, J., Daly, E., Forte, A., King, I., Yang, B. W., & Zabala, P. (2020). *Understanding the experiences and needs of Black students at Duke* [Report]. DukeSpace, Duke University Libraries. https:// dukespace.lib.duke.edu/dspace/handle/10161/ 20753

Clarke, J. H. (2012). Partnering with IT to help disadvantaged students achieve academic success. *Public Services Quarterly*, 8(3), 208–226.

Cooke, N. A. (2020, September 11). Turning antiracist knowledge and education into action. *Publisher's Weekly.* https://www.publishers weekly.com/pw/by-topic/industry-news/

libraries/article/84313-are-you-ready-to-stand-in
-the-gap.html

Crenshaw, K. (1989). Demarginalizing the intersection
of race and sex: A Black feminist critique of anti-
discrimination doctrine, feminist theory, and
antiracist politics. *University of Chicago Legal
Forum, 1989*(1), 139–167.

Cunningham, S., Guss, S., & Stout, J. (2019). Challeng-
ing the "good fit" narrative: Creating inclusive
recruitment practices in academic libraries. In
*Recasting the narrative: Proceedings of the Association
of College and Research Libraries Conference, Cleveland, OH, April 10–13, 2019* (pp. 12–21). Association of College & Research Libraries.

Department for Professional Employees, AFL-CIO.
(2020). *Library professionals: Facts and figures — 2020
Fact sheet.* https://www.dpeaflcio.org/factsheets/
library-professionals-facts-and-figures#_ednref15

DiAngelo, R. (2018). *White fragility: Why it's so hard for
white people to talk about racism.* Beacon Press.

Dunbar, A. W. (2008). *Critical race information theory:
Applying a CRITical race lens to information studies*
(Publication No. 3357343) [Doctoral dissertation,
University of California, Los Angeles]. ProQuest
Dissertations.

Duster, T. (2009, Fall). The long path to higher education for African Americans. *Thought and Action,*
99–110.

Elteto, S., Jackson, R. M., & Lim, A. (2008). Is the
library a "welcoming space"? An urban academic
library and diverse student experiences. *portal:
Libraries and the Academy, 8*(3), 325–337.

Espinal, I. (2001). A new vocabulary for inclusive
librarianship: Applying whiteness theory to our
profession. In L. Castillo-Speed (Ed.), *The power
of language = el poder de la palabra: Selected papers
from the second REFORMA national conference*
(pp. 131–149). Libraries Unlimited.

Espinal, I., Sutherland, T., & Roh, C. (2018). A holistic
approach for inclusive librarianship: Decentering

whiteness in our profession. *Library Trends, 67*(1),
147–162.

Feagin, J. R. (2020). *The White racial frame: Centuries of
framing and counter-framing (3rd ed.).* Routledge.

Folk, A. L. (2018a). Drawing on students' funds of
knowledge: Using identity and lived experience
to join the conversation in research assignments.
Journal of Information Literacy, 12(2), 44-59.

Folk, A. L. (2018b). *Learning the rules of engagement:
Exploring first-generation students' academic
experiences through academic research assignments*
(Publication No. 13819774) [Doctoral dissertation,
University of Pittsburgh]. ProQuest Dissertations.

Folk, A. L. (2021). Exploring the development of
undergraduate students' information literacy
through their experiences with research assignments. *College and Research Libraries, 82*(7).

Frueh, S. (2020, July 9). *COVID-19 and Black communities.* The National Academies of Sciences,
Engineering, and Medicine. https://www.national
academies.org/news/2020/07/covid-19-and-black
-communities

Galvan, A. (2015, June 3). Soliciting performance,
hiding bias: Whiteness and librarianship. *In the
Library with the Lead Pipe.* http://www.inthelibrary
withtheleadpipe.org/2015/soliciting-performance
-hiding-bias-whiteness-and-librarianship/

Gibson, A. N., Chancellor, R. L., Cooke, N. A., Dahlen,
S. P., Lee, S. A., & Shorish, Y. L. (2017). Libraries
on the frontlines: Neutrality and social justice.
Equality, Diversity and Inclusion, 36(8), 751–766.

Gibson, A., Hughes-Hassell, S., & Threats, M. (2018).
Critical race theory in the LIS curriculum. In
J. Percell, L. C. Sarin, P. T. Jaeger, & J. C. Bertot
(Eds.), *Re-envisioning the MLS: Perspectives on the
future of library and information science education*
(Vol. 44B, pp. 49–70). Emerald Publishing.

Gohr, M. (2017). Ethnic and racial diversity in libraries: How white allies can support arguments for
decolonization. *Journal of Radical Librarianship, 3,*
42–58.

Gorman, A. *The hill we climb: An inaugural poem for the country.* Viking Books.

Gusa, D. L. (2010). White institutional presence: The impact of whiteness on campus culture. *Harvard Educational Review*, 80(4), 464–489.

Hall, T. D. (2012). The Black body at the reference desk: Critical race theory and Black librarianship. In A. P. Jackson, J. C. Jefferson, & A. S. Nosakhere (Eds.), *The 21st-century Black librarian in America: Issues and challenges* (pp. 197–202). Scarecrow Press.

Hathcock, A. (2015). White librarianship in blackface: Diversity initiatives in LIS. *In the Library with the Lead Pipe.* https://www.inthelibrarywiththelead pipe.org/2015/lis-diversity/

Hathcock, A. M., & Sendaula, S. (2017). Mapping whiteness at the reference desk. In G. Schlesselman-Tarango (Ed.), *Topographies of Whiteness: Mapping Whiteness in library and information science* (pp. 247–256). Library Juice Press.

Hines, S. (2019). Leadership development for academic librarians: Maintaining the status quo. *Canadian Journal of Academic Librarianship*, 4, 1–19.

Holmes, B., & Lichtenstein, A. (1998). Minority student success: Librarians as partners. *College and Research Libraries News*, 59(7), 496–498.

Honma, T. (2005). Trippin' over the color line: The invisibility of race in library and information studies. *InterActions: UCLA Journal of Education and Information Studies*, 1(2), n.p.

Hudson, A. (2010). Measuring the impact of cultural diversity on desired mobile reference services. *Reference Services Review*, 38(2), 299–308.

Hudson, D. J. (2017). On "diversity" as anti-racism in library and information studies: A critique. *Journal of Critical Library and Information Studies*, 1(1), 1–36.

Katopol, P. F. (2012). Information anxiety and African-American students in a graduate education program. *Education Libraries*, 32(1/2), 5–14.

Kendi, I. X. (2020). *Be antiracist: A journal for awareness, reflection, and action.* One World.

Kendrick, K. D., & Damasco, I. T. (2019). Low morale in ethnic and racial minority academic librarians: An experiential study. *Library Trends*, 68(2), 174–212.

Kirwan Institute for the Study of Race and Ethnicity. (2018). *Implicit bias module series.* The Ohio State University. https://kirwaninstitute.osu.edu/implicit-bias-training/

Kumasi, K. (2013). "The library is like her house": Reimagining youth of color in LIS discourses. In A. Bernier (Ed.), *Transforming young adult services: A reader for our age* (pp. 103–113). ALA Neal-Schuman. Retrieved from Digital Commons@ Wayne State. http://digitalcommons.wayne.edu/slisfrp/95

Ladson-Billings, G., & Tate, W. F. (1995). Toward a critical race theory of education. *Teachers College Record*, 97(1), 47–68.

Leung, S. Y., & López-McKnight, J. R. (2020). Dreaming revolutionary futures: Critical race's centrality to ending White supremacy. *Communications in Information Literacy*, 14(1), 12–26.

Love, E. (2009). A simple step: Integrating library reference and instruction into previously established academic programs for minority students. *The Reference Librarian*, 50, 4–13.

Matthews, A. (2020). Racialized you in the public library: Systemic racism through a critical theory lens. *Theory and Research*, 15(1), 1–17.

Mortimore, J. M., & Wall, A. (2009). Motivating African-American students through information literacy instruction: Exploring the link between encouragement and academic self-concept. *Reference Librarian*, 50(1), 29–42.

Noguera, P. A. (2008). *The trouble with black boys . . . and other reflections on race, equity, and the future of public education.* Jossey Bass.

Oluo, I. (2019). *So you want to talk about race.* Seal Press.

Pashia, A. (2016). Black Lives Matter in information literacy. *Radical Teacher*, 106, 141–143.

Pawley, C. (2006). Unequal legacies: Race and multi-culturalism in the LIS curriculum. *Library Quarterly*, 76(2), 149–168.

Pierce, C. (1970). Offensive mechanisms. In F. Barbour (Ed.), *The Black seventies* (pp. 265–282). Porter Sargent.

Prescott, M. K., Caragher, K., & Dover-Taylor, K. (2017). Disrupting whiteness: Three perspectives on white anti-racist librarianship. In G. Schlessel-man-Tarango (Ed.), *Topographies of Whiteness: Mapping Whiteness in library and information science* (pp. 293–316). Library Juice Press.

Pribesh, S., Gavigan, K., & Dickinson, G. (2011). The access gap: Poverty and characteristics of school library media centers. *Library Quarterly*, 81(2), 143–160.

Project Implicit. (2011). *Project Implicit—Take a Test.* https://implicit.harvard.edu/implicit/takeatest.html

Ramirez, M. H. (2015). Being assumed not to be: A critique of Whiteness as an archival imperative. *American Archivist*, 78(2), 339–356.

Rapchak, M. (2019). That which cannot be named: The absence of race in the Framework for Information Literacy for Higher Education. *Journal of Radical Librarianship*, 5, 173–196.

Robinson, B. (2019). No holds barred: Policing and security in the public library. *In the Library with the Lead Pipe.* https://www.inthelibrarywiththeleadpipe.org/2019/no-holds-barred/

Rosa, K., & Henke, K. (2017). *2017 ALA demographic study.* American Library Association, Office for Research and Statistics. http://www.ala.org/tools/sites/ala.org.tools/files/content/Draft%20of%20Member%20Demographics%20Survey%2001-11-2017.pdf

Saad, L. F. (2020). *Me and white supremacy: Combat racism, change the world, and become a good ancestor.* Sourcebooks.

Schlesselman-Tarango, G. (2016). The legacy of Lady Bountiful: White women in the library. *Library Trends*, 64(4), 667–686.

Seidman, I. (2013). *Interviewing as qualitative research: A guide for researchers in education and the social sciences* (4th ed.). Teachers College Press.

Shachaf, P., & Snyder, M. (2007). The relationship between cultural diversity and user needs in virtual reference services. *Journal of Academic Librarianship*, 33(3), 361–367.

Shoge, R. C. (2003). The library as place in the lives of African Americans. In H. A. Thompson (Ed.), *Learning to make a difference: Proceedings of the eleventh national conference of the Association of College and Research Libraries, April 10–13, 2003, Charlotte, NC* (n.p.). Association of College & Research Libraries.

Simmons-Welburn, J., & Welburn, W. C. (2001). Cultivating partnerships/realizing diversity. *Journal of Library Administration*, 33(1/2), 5–19.

Stauffer, S.M. (2020). Educating for Whiteness: Applying critical race theory's revisionist history in library and information science research: A methodology paper. *Journal of Education for Library and Information Science*, 61(4), 452–462.

Stewart, B., Ju, B., & Kendrick, K. D. (2019). Racial climate and inclusiveness in academic libraries: Perceptions of welcomeness among Black college students. *Library Quarterly*, 89(1), 16–33.

Tatum, B. D. (2017). *Why are all the black kids sitting together in the cafeteria? And other conversations about race.* Basic Books.

van Manen, M. (1990). *Researching lived experience: Human science for an action sensitive pedagogy.* State University of New York Press.

Warner, J. N. (2001). Moving beyond Whiteness in North American academic libraries. *Libri*, 51, 167–172.

Whitmire, E. (1999). Racial differences in the academic library experiences of undergraduates. *Journal of Academic Librarianship*, 25(1), 33–37.

Whitmire, E. (2003). Cultural diversity and under-graduates' academic library use. *Journal of Academic Librarianship*, 29(3), 148–161.

Whitmire, E. (2004). The campus racial climate and undergraduates' perceptions of the academic library. *portal: Libraries and the Academy*, 4(3), 363–378.

Whitmire, E. (2006). African American undergraduates and the university academic library. *Journal of Negro Education*, 75(1), 60–66.

YALSA Young Adult Library Services Association. (n.d.). *National research agenda on libraries, learning, and teens, 2017–2021*. http://www.ala.org/yalsa/guidelines/research/researchagenda

YALSA Young Adult Library Services Association. (2015). *Teen diversity: A snapshot of U.S. teens' diversity compiled by YALSA's cultural competencies task force*. http://www.ala.org/yalsa/sites/ala.org.yalsa/files/content/TeenDemographics_Infographic.pdf

YALSA Young Adult Library Services Association. (2017). *Teen services competencies for library staff*. http://www.ala.org/yalsa/guidelines/ya competencies

Yosso, T. J. (2005). Whose culture has capital? A critical race theory discussion of community cultural wealth. *Race Ethnicity and Education*, 8(1), 69–91.

ABOUT THE AUTHORS

AMANDA L. FOLK is an associate professor and head of the Teaching and Learning department at The Ohio State University Libraries. She earned her PhD in social and comparative analysis in education from the University of Pittsburgh's School of Education. Her research interests include exploring the sociocultural nature of information literacy and implications for teaching and learning, as well as examining the academic and library experiences of student populations that have traditionally been marginalized in higher education in the United States. In addition to serving as the editor in chief for the *Journal of Academic Librarianship*, she has been published in *College and Research Libraries*, *portal: Libraries and the Academy*, *College and Undergraduate Libraries*, the *Journal of Library Administration*, and *International Information and Library Review*. She was the recipient of the 2020 ACRL Instruction Section's Ilene F. Rockman Instruction Publication of the Year Award.

TRACEY OVERBEY is assistant professor and social sciences librarian at The Ohio State University Libraries. She earned a master's degree in library and information science from the University of Pittsburgh. Her research interests include issues related to food desert communities and educating and exposing marginalized students to information literacy using library resources. She won an organizational award for implementing a seed library at The Ohio State University Libraries for students to obtain seeds from the library to plant fresh produce within their residence halls. This initiative helped those students and faculty who live in food desert communities. She has also won state and local grants that expose students who live within economically strained communities to science, technology, engineering, and math (STEM) resources through programming and hands-on explorations. In addition, she serves on the Executive Board for the Black Caucus of the American Library Association, has published in *Public Library Quarterly* and *International Journal of Environmental Health Research*, and has presented papers at conferences of the International Federation of Library Associations (IFLA) and the Association of College and Research Libraries (ACRL).

INDEX